SpringerBriefs in Population Studies

Population Studies of Japan

The world population is expected to expand by 39.4% to 9.6 billion in 2060 (UN World Population Prospects, revised 2010). Meanwhile, Japan is expected to see its population contract by nearly one third to 86.7 million, and its proportion of the elderly (65 years of age and over) will account for no less than 39.9% (National Institute of Population and Social Security Research in Japan, Population Projections for Japan 2012). Japan has entered the post-demographic transitional phase and will be the fastest-shrinking country in the world, followed by former Eastern bloc nations, leading other Asian countries that are experiencing drastic changes.

A declining population that is rapidly aging impacts a country's economic growth, labor market, pensions, taxation, health care, and housing. The social structure and geographical distribution in the country will drastically change, and short-term as well as long-term solutions for economic and social consequences of this trend will be required.

This series aims to draw attention to Japan's entering the post-demographic transition phase and to present cutting-edge research in Japanese population studies. It will include compact monographs under the editorial supervision of the Population Association of Japan (PAJ).

The PAJ was established in 1948 and organizes researchers with a wide range of interests in population studies of Japan. The major fields are (1) population structure and aging; (2) migration, urbanization, and distribution; (3) fertility; (4) mortality and morbidity; (5) nuptiality, family, and households; (6) labor force and unemployment; (7) population projection and population policy (including family planning); and (8) historical demography. Since 1978, the PAJ has been publishing the academic journal *Jinkogaku Kenkyu* (The Journal of Population Studies), in which most of the articles are written in Japanese.

Thus, the scope of this series spans the entire field of population issues in Japan, impacts on socioeconomic change, and implications for policy measures. It includes population aging, fertility and family formation, household structures, population health, mortality, human geography and regional population, and comparative studies with other countries.

This series will be of great interest to a wide range of researchers in other countries confronting a post-demographic transition stage, demographers, population geographers, sociologists, economists, political scientists, health researchers, and practitioners across a broad spectrum of social sciences.

More information about this subseries at http://www.springer.com/series/13101

Hisakazu Kato

Macro-econometric Analysis on Determinants of Fertility Behavior

Springer

Hisakazu Kato
School of Political Science and Economics
Meiji University
Tokyo, Japan

ISSN 2211-3215 ISSN 2211-3223 (electronic)
SpringerBriefs in Population Studies
ISSN 2198-2724 ISSN 2198-2732 (electronic)
Population Studies of Japan
ISBN 978-981-16-3926-5 ISBN 978-981-16-3927-2 (eBook)
https://doi.org/10.1007/978-981-16-3927-2

This Springer imprint is published by the registered company Springer Nature Singapore Pte Ltd.
The registered company address is: 152 Beach Road, #21-01/04 Gateway East, Singapore 189721, Singapore

Acknowledgements

I would like to appreciate the editors and reviewers of *SpringerBriefs in Population Studies, Population Studies of Japan*, in particular Prof. Toshihiko Hara (Sapporo City University). He kindly advised my work from multi-perspectives. As always, any remaining errors are my own. I also would like to thank the members of Population Association of Japan because I learned a lot of knowledge from the activities in Population Association of Japan. In addition, I would like to thank Yutaka Hirachi for editing this book. Lastly, I want to dedicate this book to my late father.

Introduction

The total fertility rate (TFR) in Japan has been declining since the mid-1970s, and it reached 1.26 in 2005, the lowest level since World War II. Although the TFR rose slightly thereafter, it was still just 1.32 in 2019, which is much low level from the perspective of the maintenance of the current population size.

The causes of declining TFR have been discussed for a long time in the past, and it would be difficult to point out only a few factors that determine the decline in TFR. Many social and economic matters are related to fertility change.

The purpose of this book is to explore the economic and social determinant factors of fertility behavior holistically. Though many previous researches about empirical analysis of fertility behavior and the related demographic events, but this research has three characteristics. The first is that the relationship between fertility and labor participation by female is considered thoroughly, because there are discussions about structural change between them. The second is that various types of models such as Bayesian vector autoregressive (BVAR) model or dynamic panel model are applied to explore the determinant factors of fertility behavior. The third is that we confirm the effectiveness of public policies related to improve fertility rate.

This book is made up of three chapters, and each chapter is assigned various type data, such as time series, cross section, and panel data. In recent years, micro-econometric analysis has become popular; however, this book has another approach from the perspective of macro- or semi–macroeconometrics.

The title and overviews are as follows:

Chapter 1: "Low Fertility and Female Labor Supply in Japan—Time Series Analysis Using Bayesian VAR Approach."
This chapter empirically interprets the dynamic relationship between the TFR, female wage, and labor participation from the time series perspective, using Japan's experience. Our research results show that female wages negatively impact the fertility rate by using BVAR model. This can be interpreted that women's wages are an opportunity cost of having children, and we reconfirmed this fact in Japan's experience. Furthermore, adding the government benefits to young families to the BVAR model shows that this positively affects the TFR by calculating

impulse response function. Hence, the intervention by the government to improve the TFR is appropriate.

Chapter 2: "Analysis of the Regional Disparity in the Total Fertility Rate in Japan—From the Perspective of Population Density and Socioeconomic Factors." This chapter examines the background of the disparity in the TFR at the municipality level. The large regional disparity in the TFR is driven by the differences in child-related costs, the work/life balance between employment and child-rearing for young families, the existence of a young population, and the policies of municipalities. Using the TFR data in 2015 of Japan's municipalities, we examined the relationship between the TFR and socioeconomic variables. We find that the coefficient of population density is negative and that of the female labor force participation rate is positive, and both are statistically significant. These findings suggest that children-related costs negatively influence the TFR. Additionally, the government's policy for raising the TFR positively affects the TFR.

Chapter 3: "Total Fertility Rate, Economic–Social Conditions, and Public Policies in OECD Countries."

A long-term decline trend in the TFR has been observed in almost all the OECD countries. This chapter explores these common factors which affect declining TFR using balanced panel data for OECD countries from 1986 to 2017. Especially, we focus four kinds of variables such as labor market, macroeconomic environments, political tools, and demographic conditions. We find that while the female labor participation (FLP) rate correlates positively with TFR, the female unemployment rate (FUR) negatively impacts TFR. The GDP per capita affects TFR negatively; on the other side, the economic growth rate positively affects the TFR. Furthermore, while the coefficient of the length of maternity and parental leave has negative signs, social expenditure has a positive influence on the TFR.

Contents

Chapter 1
Low Fertility and Female Labor Supply in Japan—Time Series Analysis Using Bayesian VAR Approach

Abstract Japanese society faces a low fertility rate and population decline, and the declining population brings about a shortage of labor forces. Therefore, female labor participation is attracting attention. However, cross-sectional data show a positive relationship between the total fertility rate (TFR) and female labor participation in recent years, while the time series data suggest a negative relationship. This may be a puzzle waiting to be solved. This chapter empirically interprets the dynamic relationship between the TFR, female wage, and labor participation from the time series perspective, using Japan's experience. Generally, the VAR model is used to confirm the dynamic relationship among relevant variables; however, it is not easy to use the VAR model because the variables have a unit root. This study verifies the dynamic relationship using the error correction model (ECM) and Bayesian vector autoregression (BVAR) models. Therefore, both ECM and BVAR models show a similar result. They show that female wages negatively impact the fertility rate, and a similar result was obtained from both ECM and BVAR models. Women's wages are an opportunity cost of having children, and we reconfirmed this fact in Japan's experience. Additionally, this means that the compatible situation for women between labor provision and rearing children has been insufficient in Japan. Furthermore, adding the government benefits to young families to the BVAR model shows that this positively affects the TFR by calculating impulse response function. This can be interpreted as the government benefits reducing the opportunity cost of children. Hence, the intervention by the government to improve the TFR is appropriate.

Keywords Fertility rate · Female's labor participation · ECM · Bayesian VAR

1.1 Introduction

Many developed countries are suffering from low birth rate, and Japan is no exception. Japan's total fertility rate (TFR) has been consistently below 2.0 since the mid-1970s, and the risks and problems of such a low fertility rate have been seriously discussed from the early 1990s. Not only in Japan, but also in other East Asian countries, the low level of birth is remarkable.

H. Kato, *Macro-econometric Analysis on Determinants of Fertility Behavior*, Population Studies of Japan, https://doi.org/10.1007/978-981-16-3927-2_1

East Asian Miracle is the well-known phenomenon, and South Korea, Taiwan, Hong Kong, and Singapore had experienced rapid and high economic growth till the mid-1990s. In parallel with such economic growth of four countries, birth rate also has been declining greatly. Therefore, empirical studies on the factors behind the low fertility rate in Japan will be referable for other Asian countries as well. In this book, we focus the relationship between fertility rate and female labor provision in main, because the time series trend of this relationship is almost common in East Asian countries.

With regard to Japan's fertility rate, in 2005, the TFR recorded its lowest levels since the World War II, after which it increased slightly to 1.45 in 2015. In 2019, the TFR in Japan was 1.36, which is much lower than the replacement ratio to maintain the number of current populations. In addition, it is expected that COVID-19 will bring further reduce of fertility in near future.

From the economic perspectives, there are vast studies and some theories that try to explain the relationship between economic growth and low fertility; for example, Becker (1960) or Leibenstein (1957) is a typical and classical reference. Many past studies emphasize the "cost" of having children to understand low fertility problem. Hence, considering the low fertility phenomenon in developed countries, opportunity cost of children is an important factor, and this is closely related to female labor provision. In other words, considering children as durable goods, their costs and family income are fundamental factors that need to be analyzed. In particular, the opportunity cost of a child for a woman, that is, the loss of her lifelong income due to renouncing her job in order to rear her child, is the most essential factor, and this is influenced by her wages. From this perspective, the decision by woman whether to have a child or whether to continue supplying her labor has a close relationship.

There are literatures that have studied influences of female wages as opportunity cost of child to fertility. Willis (1973) gave theoretical basis of the above opportunity cost using household production function. The most referred empirical study about opportunity cost is Mincer (1963), which showed that increase in wages made number of births fewer in the USA. Furthermore, Butz and Ward (1979) developed a more realistic model for empirical analysis, and they found that fertility rate was influenced by business cycle inversely and wife's wage negatively affected fertility rate.

However, female labor participation (or female's social position) is also an important factor to consider the change in fertility rate. Past decades, it was observed that the relation between total fertility rate (TFR) and female's labor participation rate was negative in cross-sectional analysis. However, in recent years this relation has changed to positive [see Ahn and Mira (2002) or D'Addio and D'Ercole (2005)]. And in time series data, again negative relationship is still observed.

Discussions about correlation between female's labor participation and TFR continue; however, the true reason of that has not been explained yet. Many studies tried to show that the true mechanism existed, but we have not arrived at the complete understandings of that. Kato (2020) tried to investigate this relationship in case of Japan using structural VAR model. To scrutinize these relationships, we try to analyze interdependence among those variables in Japan using Bayesian VAR model.

The main purpose of this study is to give an empirical interpretation about the relation among TFR, female's wage, and labor participation from time series perspective using Japan's experience. In order to achieve this purpose, we will estimate the VAR model and measure impulse response functions using Bayesian inference.

This chapter is organized as follows. Section 1.2 summarizes the trends of TFR decline and introduces the discussion of causes of declining TFR. Section 1.3 provides literatures on low fertility in developed countries from the perspective of economics. Section 1.4 discusses time series characteristics of the data and estimation strategy of ECM and Bayesian VAR model. Section 1.5 shows the estimation results and the interpretations from these models. Furthermore, in Sect. 1.6, we consider the effect of government intervention to TFR. Concluding remarks and policy implications is given in Sect. 1.7.

1.2 Low Fertility in Japan

1.2.1 Trend of TFR in Japan

Figure 1.1 shows the long-term trend in the TFR in Japan. During the period immediately after the World War II, Japan's total fertility rate was very high, because young ex-soldiers had returned from foreign countries, resulting in a "baby boom" situation. Therefore, TFR was as high as 4.54 in 1947 and 4.40 in 1948. This high TFR gradually decreased with the acceleration in economic growth, a general trend observed in developed countries. By 1961, the TFR in Japan had declined to 1.96. The reasons for decline in TFR in developed countries have been discussed by various researchers

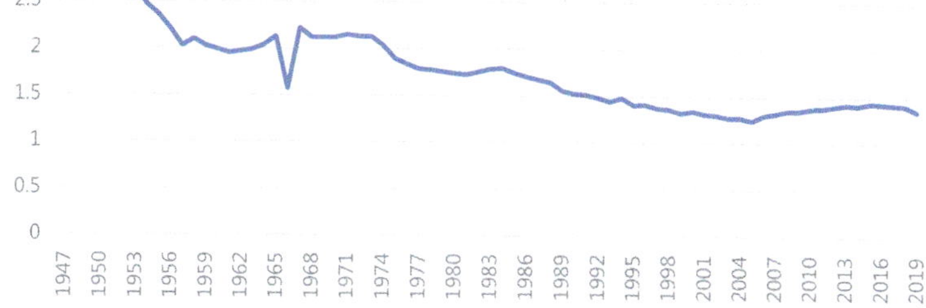

Fig. 1.1 Trends of TFR in long-term periods. *Source* Ministry of Health, Labour and Welfare "Vital Statistics"

including Leibenstein (1957) and Becker (1960), whose contribution in this field was seminal. As regards Japan, it experienced a sudden temporary drop in TFR to 1.58 in 1966, owing to a traditional superstition called "hinoe uma," after which it recovered slightly. However, from the latter half of the 1970s, the TFR started to decline again as Japan's economy entered a new era of lower economic growth compared to the earlier high economic growth era.

Since the latter half of the 1970s, female labor supply began to increase, while the TFR continued to decline. This elicited widespread debate on the negative relationship between the two variables. In 1990, the "1.57 shock" occurred triggering social concern, because the previous year's TFR was lower than 1.58 in 1966, hinoe uma year.

After the collapse of the bubble economy in Japan, the TFR continued to decline, but at a faster pace of decline in the 1990s and the first half of the 2000s. The TFR recorded a historical low of 1.26 in 2005, the lowest after the World War II. In the latter half of the 2000s, the TFR gradually improved and reached 1.45 in 2015, before declining marginally to 1.36 in 2019. Even though the prediction of TFR is difficult, relating it to factors such as female labor supply or economic growth can help improve TFR prediction.

1.2.2 Cause of Declining TFR

The causes of declining TFR have been discussed for a longtime in the past, and it would be difficult to point out only a few factors that determine the decline in TFR. Many social and economic matters are related to fertility change, and we need to explore this issue holistically.

With respect to the demographic aspect, Japan's tradition links marriage and birth, and change in marriage behavior affects change in TFR. Specifically, the number of late marriages or individuals remaining unmarried has increased in the past four decades, resulting in a decline in the TFR. The first marriage age of females has been increasing since the middle of the 1970s—the mean age of the first marriage of a female was 25.2 years in 1980, 27.0 years in 2000, and 29.6 years in 2019. In addition, the marital status has also drastically changed—the ratio of currently married women to total female population aged 25–29 years was 24.0% in 1980 as compared to 61.3% in 2015. Late marriage leads to late birth, and demographers stress this change of marriage behavior as the most important factor determining the trends in TFR. Therefore, they recommend promoting marriage as a priority policy to improve the TFR.

Economists consider socioeconomic conditions as more important factors affecting fertility changes. Firstly, the cost of children, which includes educational cost, has been increasing with economic development, a common phenomenon in developed countries. Secondly, the opportunity cost of a child for a woman also increases as female labor supply increases, which is one of the key objectives of this study. Under inadequate institutional or policy support system for child-rearing and jobs for married women, those women who give up their jobs in order to take care of their children might lose lifelong earnings. To this extent, this can be considered as the opportunity cost of children. Economists point out this opportunity cost as the most important factor affecting both marriage and childbearing behavior of young females. This issue was raised by Becker (1960) and Willis (1973).

Furthermore, labor market conditions and job status are also necessary factors to be considered in case of young families trying to have children. As described at the above section, the TFR declined rapidly in the 1990s and the first half of the 2000s. This decline in TFR was reflected in deteriorating labor market conditions for youth and increasing nonregular workers whose income was lower than regular worker. Thus, it is said that the unstable condition of youth was one of the factors that led to the decline in TFR during this period.

There are other factors to decline in TFR. For example, the traditional role of children, which supported the daily life of retired parents, is substituted by modern pension system, thereby reducing the incentive of having children. Further, a pessimistic economic expectation of the future among the young people, or the change in their values of marriage and having children, should also be considered. Although there are numerous elements affecting the change in TFR during past decades in Japan, we will analyze only a few factors which seem to be strongly related to TFR.

1.3 Literature on Low Fertility in Developed Countries

1.3.1 Opportunity Cost or Female Wage and TFR

From an economic perspective, costs play an important role in the decision-making of having children. In particular, the opportunity cost plays a decisive role. There is a large body of literature that studies the influence of female wages on the opportunity cost of child and fertility. Willis (1973) gave a theoretical basis of the above opportunity cost using household production function. The most referred empirical study on the opportunity cost is Mincer (1963), which showed that increase in wages reduced the number of births in the USA. Furthermore, Butz and Ward (1979) developed a concrete model for estimation and found that fertility rate was inversely influenced by business cycle and a wife's wage negatively affected the fertility rate.

Butz–Ward-type model was estimated by many researchers, and there are also many papers using Japan's data. First, Ogawa and Mason (1986) described the statistically negative impact of the increase in opportunity costs on the TFR using time series data from 1966 to 1984. They found a positive relationship between husband's income and TFR, which is called the income effect for TFR. On the other hand, there are papers that disagreed the applicability of Butz–Ward model to Japanese TFR; for example, Imai (1996) or Kato (1997) rejected the implications of opportunity cost on fertility rate as being statistically meaningful. However, Butz–Ward model dealt with only static and simultaneous relationship; hence, the estimation model has to consider a dynamic path of female wage to TFR to obtain more robust conclusion. Furthermore, Toda (2007) set estimation model which adopted the basic concept of opportunity cost and concluded that relative wage of female in general had a negative effect on TFR using panel data of Japan's prefectures. Also, Suzuki (2018) used panel data of Japan's prefectures from 1965 to 2015 and showed that increase in female wages had a negative impact on fertility. However, this conclusion was not robust in the case of 1985 to 2015 subperiod.

1.3.2 Female Labor Participation and TFR

Discussions about correlation between female labor participation and TFR still continue. One of the contributions of this study is to make clear the relationship between female labor participation and TFR. It is well known that the sign of correlation between them had changed from negative to positive in developed countries around the 1980s (Fig. 1.2), although the true reason for this has not been explained yet. Many researches have tried to show this mechanism; however, we are yet to completely understand it.

Ahn and Mira (2002) may have been the first paper that raised this issue, followed by Engelhardt et al. (2004) and Kőgel (2004). Furthermore, D'Addio and D'Ercole (2005) presented the annual trends in the sign of the correlation coefficient from 1980 to 1999 using data from 22 OECD countries. Figure 1.2 is from D'Addio and D'Ercole (2005), and it illustrates that the sign of correlation coefficient had changed around the latter half of the 1980s. Engelhardt et al. (2004) raised this issue using cross-country comparison of macrolevel time series data and estimating error correction model (ECM) and concluded that social norms, social institutions, or financial incentives influenced the change in sign of correlation between female's labor participation and TFR. On the other hand, Kőgel (2004) claimed that the changing sign was affected by

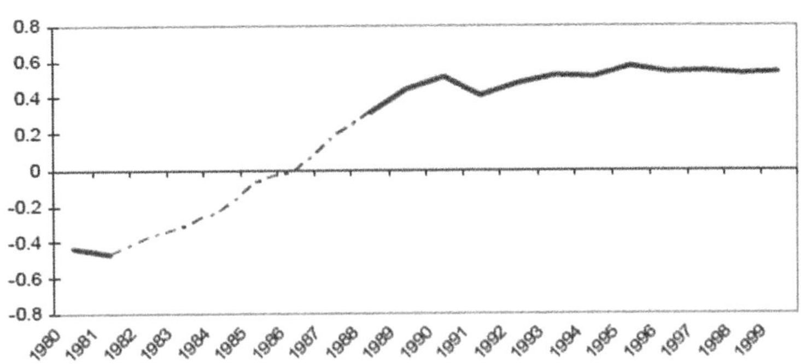

Fig. 1.2 Correlation between female employment rates and total fertility rates in OECD countries over the 1980–1999. *Source* D'Addio and D'Ercole (2005)

the presence of unmeasured country-specific factors in panel data analysis. Mishra and Smyth (2014) tackled this issue applying methods of time series analysis such as panel unit root or panel cointegration. They claimed that measuring a sign of female's labor force participation and the total fertility rate depended on the time period and how the female labor force participation rate is measured.

Recently, Jaba et al. (2016) picked up this issue again and reconfirmed the existence of relationship between the female employment rate and TFR. However, they concluded that the relationship between them behaved differently among EU countries and depended on specific labor market characteristics, including political regimes and geographical aspects. Shastri (2015) also estimated this relationship and reconfirmed the existence of negative relationship because of high level of incompatibility between the roles of a mother and a worker at that time.

In Japan, the Cabinet Office (2005) showed the scatterplot of female's labor participation rate and TFR in OECD countries during 1970, 1985, and 2000, and described that the propensity in relationship of both was changed. Yamaguchi (2005) studied this complicated problem and found that the progress in support for balancing childcare and employment of females had resulted in changing a sign of correlation between them. Lee and Lee (2014) considered the relationship and causality between childcare availability and female labor force participation rate, and found that there was no evidence which suggests that working women tend to have fewer children.

1.4 Data and Analytical Model

1.4.1 Data

To analyze the relationship between TFR and other economic–social factors, such as female's labor participation rate, wage indicator, and economic prosperity, we chose four variables as follows: FLP2554, WAGE, WAGEGAP, and GDPG. The sources of data are as follows: TFR is from "Vital Statistics" by the Ministry of Health, Labour and Welfare, FLP2554, which is 25–54 year-old women's labor participation rate, and is from "Labor Force Survey" by the Ministry of Internal Affairs and Communications, Statistics Bureau. We used labor participation rate instead of employment rate because we want to measure the possibility of labor supply of women, and employment rate is influenced by other economic conditions. WAGE is from "Basic Survey on Wage Structure" by the Ministry of Health, Labour and Welfare, and WAGE is measured by contractual average cash earnings of women (both regular and nonregular workers) every month, and the unit is thousand yen. LWAGE is taking logarithm of WAGE. WAGEGAP is the ratio of female's wage to male's wage. Increase in wage gap may bring heavier opportunity cost regarding a child for women, who cannot enjoy the compatible support with childcare and labor provision. Lastly, GDPG is from the "Annual Report on National Accounts" by the Cabinet Office. All variables are available from 1980 to 2019. Figure 1.3 shows the transition of these variables.

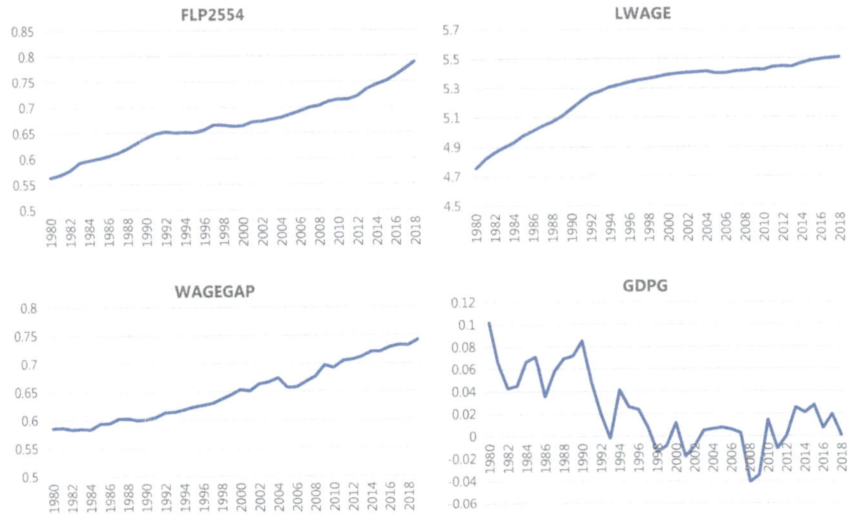

Fig. 1.3 Main independent. *Source* See text

1.4.2 Pre-estimation Results

In general, in case of estimating time series data in each country including Japan, the result would be ambiguously showing a negative relation before the 1990s and a positive relation thereafter. As for the estimated correlation coefficient change that D'Addio and D'Ercole (2005) showed, it could be considered as a result of a structural change that occurred in the past. The simplest method to deal with data whose structure changed is to divide sample period at the time when structural change occurred. However, there are two difficult problems. One to fix the time when structural change occurred is much difficult; another is that it is difficult to collect enough amount of data that can provide statistically reliable result. So, it is difficult to gain clear and time-invariant results from time series data.

Table 1.1 shows the simple regression result using TFR, labor participation rate (FLP2554), female wage (WAGE), and economic growth rate (GDPG). Table 1.1 requires a rather complicate interpretation of result of Eq. (1.1); that is, FLP2554 has negative coefficient to TFR. However, Eqs. (1.3) and (1.4) added WAGE or/and GDPG as independent variables to Eq. (1.1), the sign of coefficient of FLP2554 turns positive, and coefficient of WAGE turns negative. Both coefficients are statistically significant. It is required to interpret these results.

If WAGE is the endogenous variable that affects both TFR and labor simultaneously, then we should deal with problem of endogeneity in Eqs. (1.3) and (1.4); that is, to avoid endogeneity in estimation, GMM estimation is the appropriate method. Instead of OLS estimation, Eqs. (1.5) and (1.6) are estimated by GMM, that is, 2SLS method, and signs of estimated coefficient of independent variable are the same as Eqs. (1.3) and (1.4). From these results, we should consider the model which includes

Table 1.1 Regression result of TFR and labor participation rate of female

	Equation (1.1)	Equation (1.2)	Equation (1.3)	Equation (1.4)	Equation (1.5)	Equation (1.6)
Const	2.778***	2.797***	6.148***	5.8704***	6.5262***	6.1641***
	(0.2118)	(0.4495)	(0.2741)	(0.4255)	(0.4503)	(0.5975)
FLP2554	−1.9315***	−1.9607***	1.6828***	1.5970***	1.8561***	1.7391***
	(0.3134)	(0.6637)	(0.3082)	(0.3252)	(0.4168)	(0.4253)
LWAGE	–	–	−1.0976***	−1.0357***	−1.1901***	−1.1086***
	–	–	(0.0843)	(0.1113)	(0.1304)	(0.1588)
LGDP	–	–	–	0.3460	–	0.4295
	–	–	–	−0.4045	–	(0.3773)
Method	OLS	GMM	OLS	OLS	GMM	GMM
Period	1980–2019	1981–2019	1980–2019	1980–2019	1981–2019	1981–2019
Adj. R^2	0.4865	0.4488	0.9056	0.9049	0.9197	0.9214

Note *** means 1% statistically significant, and * means 10% significant
As for GMM estimation, instrumental variables are mainly lagged independent variables.
All variables except TFR are transformed to natural logged values

3 variables, namely TFR, labor, and wage. In addition, to grasp time lagged effect in each variable to the other variables, we should adopt a more dynamic model such as the VAR model. In addition, when these variables in OLS equation are not stationary, results of Table 1.1 may be spurious regression. Hence, we should confirm the time series characteristics in all variables.

1.4.3 Time Series Characteristics

Figure 1.3 shows the four variables, and all variables including TFR except GDPG seem to have upward or downward trend; therefore, we should confirm the stationarity of these variables. Hence, unit root test is required to confirm stationarity of each variable.

Table 1.2 shows the results of unit root test. ADF test with intercept is adopted, but other tests, such as DF–GLS test or Ng-Perron modified test, bring almost the same results. Optimal lag length of unit root test is determined by AIC criterion using full sample of each variable.

From Table 1.2, it cannot be rejected to have unit root in all variables except GDPG. For example, ADF statistics of TFR is −2.0537, and the probability of having unit root is 26.4%; then, we cannot reject the hypothesis that TFR has unit root. Furthermore, we take first difference of series of each variable and test it about unit root. As a result, the differenced series of FLP2554, LWAGE, and WAGEGAP does not have unit root, but TFR cannot reject the hypothesis of unit root. However, the differenced TFR series is difficult to interpret in the economic meanings; subsequently, we will deal with all variables as I (1) (the order of integration is one) variable.

Table 1.2 Results of unit root test (ADF test with intercept)

	TFR	FLP2554	WAGEGAP	LWAGE	GDPG
Level					
Statistics	−2.0537	1.108	0.8212	−2.7011*	−3.023**
Probability	0.2638	0.9969	0.9932	0.0832	0.041
Lag length	2	2	0	1	1
Differenced					
Statistics	−2.7576	−3.2574**	−7.0781***	−2.9796**	−6.3352***
Probability	0.2211	0.0242	0	0.0459	0.0000
Lag length	1	0	0	0	1

Note Null hypothesis is each variable has a unit root
*** denotes significance at the 1% level, ** denotes significance at 5% level, and * denotes significance at 10% level
Sample period: 1980–2019
Lag length is chosen by AIC

1.4.4 Strategy of Empirical Analysis

We cannot deal with all variable as stationary; therefore, the existence of cointegration should be confirmed as the standard step to deal with time series analysis, and when there is cointegration among the variables, then error correction model (ECM) is adopted to observe the long-term relationship. If there would be no cointegration, then VAR model could be estimated by the differenced series; however, differenced VAR model loses the information, which level variable holds.

We can propose another step to estimate VAR model using I (1) variables by Bayesian approach, since Bayesian VAR (BVAR) model can deal with unit root variables as prior information. Note that there is another discussion, which is interested in the natures of relationships between variables, not accurate parameter value, estimating VAR with nonstationary variables that may give important insights (Sims (1980)).

In addition, we have a much difficult estimation problem, that is, shortage of degree of freedom to estimate ECM or VAR model. For example, if we adopt 2 lags with 4 variables in each equation in VAR model, and we have only 40 data in each variable, then the degree of freedom will reduce to 31, which is insufficient to make standard statistical inference. One of the benefits adopting BVAR is providing a logical way of introducing shrinkage of estimation coefficients (see Koop and Korobilis (2009), Kuschnig and Vashold (2019), etc.). In this study, the Minnesota prior is adopted as prior distribution to estimate BVAR model, and the Minnesota prior can lead to analytical results for posterior densities. In other words, natural conjugate prior, such as the Minnesota prior, can bring analytical computation and reduce computational burden instead of Markov chain Monte Carlo (MCMC) method.

1.4.5 Cointegration

To observe the dynamical relationship among variables, which are I (1) variables, ECM gives us useful information, if cointegration among variables exists. Before estimating ECM, we should confirm cointegration by Johansen's test.

Cointegration is the popular concept when analyzing time series data. It is known that many time series data have unit root, that is, I (1) variable. When $x_1, x_2, \ldots, x_k$ are I (1) variables, and the linear combination

$$\beta_1 x_{1t} + \beta_2 x_{2t} + \cdots + \beta_k x_{kt} = \boldsymbol{\beta x}_t$$

becomes stationary, then it is said that these variables have cointegration. Note that the variables are not distinction between endogenous and exogeneous variables. If there is cointegration among variables, this is interpreted that they have common trend in the long run.

Table 1.3 Result of Johansen cointegration test

No. of Co.	Eigenvalue	Trace statistics	Probability	Max eigen. stat	Probability
Variable: TFR, FLP2554, LWAGE					
$r = 0$*	0.3469	31.0029	0.0362	16.1899	0.2140
$r = 1$	0.2414	14.8130	0.0632	10.4972	0.1813
$r = 2$*	0.1074	4.3157	0.0378	4.3157	0.0378
Variable: TFR, FLP2554, WAGEGAP					
$r = 0$	0.3235	28.1334	0.0768	14.8537	0.2993
$r = 1$	0.2204	13.2797	0.1049	9.4600	0.2499
$r = 2$	0.0956	3.8197	0.0506	3.8197	0.0506

Note * denotes rejection of the hypothesis at the 0.05 level
Lag interval (in first difference):1 to 1

After the estimation of ECM, it can calculate error correction term, which describes long-run movement toward the equilibrium among the variables. ECM is described as

$$\Delta \boldsymbol{x}_t = \Pi \boldsymbol{x}_{t-1} + \sum_{j=1}^{p-1} \Gamma_t \Delta \boldsymbol{x}_{t-1} + \boldsymbol{\varepsilon}_t \tag{1.1}$$

and error correction term is $\Pi \boldsymbol{x}_{t-1}$. We will note the coefficient of error correction term Π, and this is rewritten as $\Pi = \alpha\beta'$, where $\boldsymbol{\alpha}$ is called as loading matrix, which describes the speed to its long-run equilibrium.

Table 1.3 shows the results of the cointegration tests for (TFR, FLP2554, LWAGE) and (TFR, FLP2554, WAGEGAP) using Johansen's method. Note that we excluded GDPG in cointegration test, because GDPG seems stationary from Table 1.2. In case of combination (TFR, FLP2554, LWAGE), both Trace Test and Max-eigenvalue Test results reject null hypothesis of no cointegration at 1% statistically significance. However, we could not obtain cointegration of combination (TFR, FLP2554, WAGEGAP). From this result, we assumed the existence of cointegration in (TFR, FLP2554, LWAGE) and will estimate ECM later.

1.4.6 Bayesian VAR Model

In recent year, VAR model has become a popular tool to capture the dynamics of linear multiple time series data. However, as explained the above, shortage of degree of freedom in equations is a severe problem. Bayesian inference changes the estimation frame work, treats the coefficient of equation as a random variable, and estimates posterior distribution. The posterior distribution is calculated by combining information provided by a sample of observed data and prior information. In other words, how the prior information is provided is an important part to estimate BVAR model. In this study, we utilize the Minnesota prior, which is one of the most adopted priors for the VAR model, and this assumes the belief that each variable has unit root.

We define VAR model as

$$\boldsymbol{y}_t = \boldsymbol{a}_0 + \sum_{j=1}^{p} \boldsymbol{A}_j \boldsymbol{y}_{t-j} + \boldsymbol{\varepsilon}_t \tag{1.2}$$

where $\boldsymbol{y}_t$: M $\times$ 1 matrix, $\boldsymbol{A}_j$: M $\times$ M matrix, $\boldsymbol{\varepsilon}_t$: M $\times$ 1 matrix, and $\boldsymbol{\varepsilon}_t \sim i.i.d.N(0, \Sigma_{\boldsymbol{\varepsilon}})$.

We can express as

$$\boldsymbol{X} = \begin{bmatrix} \boldsymbol{x}_1 \\ \boldsymbol{x}_2 \\ \vdots \\ \boldsymbol{x}_T \end{bmatrix} \quad \boldsymbol{x}_t = \begin{bmatrix} 1 \ \boldsymbol{y}'_{t-1} \ \boldsymbol{y}'_{t-2} \cdots \boldsymbol{y}'_{t-p} \end{bmatrix} \quad : (1 + MP) \text{ vector.}$$

$\boldsymbol{y}$ and $\boldsymbol{\varepsilon}$ is stack matrix of $\boldsymbol{y}_t$ and $\boldsymbol{\varepsilon}_t$,

$$\boldsymbol{A} = \begin{bmatrix} \boldsymbol{\alpha}_0 \\ \boldsymbol{A}_1 \\ \vdots \\ \boldsymbol{A}_p \end{bmatrix} \text{ and } \boldsymbol{\theta} = vec(\boldsymbol{A}).$$

then,

$$\boldsymbol{y} = (\boldsymbol{I}_m \otimes \boldsymbol{X})\boldsymbol{\theta} + \boldsymbol{\varepsilon} \tag{1.3}$$

In Minnesota prior, assuming $\boldsymbol{\theta}$ obeys a normal prior with fixed $\Sigma_{\boldsymbol{\varepsilon}}$; in other words, $\Sigma_{\boldsymbol{\varepsilon}}$ is known and is estimated by OLS in each equation or by maximum likelihood (ML) method in full VAR. Therefore, we can describe $\widehat{\sum}_{\boldsymbol{\varepsilon}}$ as estimator of $\sum_{\boldsymbol{\varepsilon}}$.

Subsequently, we assume prior distribution of $\boldsymbol{\theta}$ as

$$\boldsymbol{\theta} \sim \boldsymbol{N}(\boldsymbol{\theta}_0, \ \boldsymbol{V}_0) \tag{1.4}$$

and assume $\boldsymbol{\theta}_0 = 0, \quad \boldsymbol{V}_0 \neq 0$. Furthermore, $\boldsymbol{V}_0$ is set as

$$v_{ij}^l = \begin{matrix} \left(\frac{\lambda_1}{l\lambda^3}\right)^2 & \text{for } i = j \\ \left(\frac{\lambda_1 \lambda_2 \sigma_i}{l\lambda^3 \sigma_j}\right)^2 & \text{for } i \neq j \end{matrix} \; l = 1, \ldots, p. \tag{1.5}$$

where σ_i^2 is the ith diagonal element of $\Sigma_{\boldsymbol{\varepsilon}}$.

Here, we can define hyper-parameter $\lambda_1, \lambda_2, \ \lambda_3$, and this hyper-parameter determines the character of prior. According to define the prior, the posterior distribution of θ is obtained analytically as follows:

$$\theta \sim N\left(\bar{\theta},\ \bar{V}\right) \tag{1.6}$$

where
$\overline{V} = \left[V_0^{-1} + \left(\widehat{\sum_{\varepsilon}}^{-1} \otimes X'X\right)\right]^{-1}, \overline{\theta} = \overline{V}\left[V_0^{-1}\theta_0 + \left(\widehat{\sum_{\varepsilon}}^{-1} \otimes X\right)' y\right].$

1.5 Estimation Results and Findings

1.5.1 Ordinary VAR Estimation

Firstly, whether each series has unit root or not, we estimated ordinary VAR model, which is constructed by four-variable model with 1 lag. As for determining the lag length, we obtained from some information criterions. Equation for TFR is as follows

$$\begin{aligned} \text{TFR} = {} & \underset{(0.0976)}{0.6849} \times \text{TFR}(-1) + \underset{(0.2718)}{0.7810} \times \text{FLP2554}(-1) - \underset{(0.1247)}{0.4438} \times \text{LWAGE}(-1) \\ & - \underset{(0.2305)}{0.5127} \times \text{GDPG}(-1) + \underset{(0.6323)}{2.2893} \end{aligned} \tag{1.7}$$

(Standard errors are in parentheses)

This result suggests that LWAGE and GDPG negatively affect TFR; on the other hand, FLP2554 positively affects TFR in statistically significant. This means TFR has a declining property as women's wage rising in labor market. From this estimation of VAR model, the impulse response functions can be calculated as Fig. 1.4 shows.

Impulse response functions are calculated using Cholesky decomposition. External shock to LWAGE reduces TFR and is statistically significant. In other words, a positive shock to female wage brings negative impact on TFR. On the other hand, a positive shock to FLP2554 leads to a positive impact on TFR. Furthermore, the impact on LWAGE leads to a negative impact on FLP2554; hence, it is interpreted that the substitution effect of wage on labor participation is estimated in our calculation.

1.5.2 Error Correction Model

As described above, the existence of cointegration is not rejected; hence, we estimate VECM using the result of Johansen test. The error correction term of VECM is

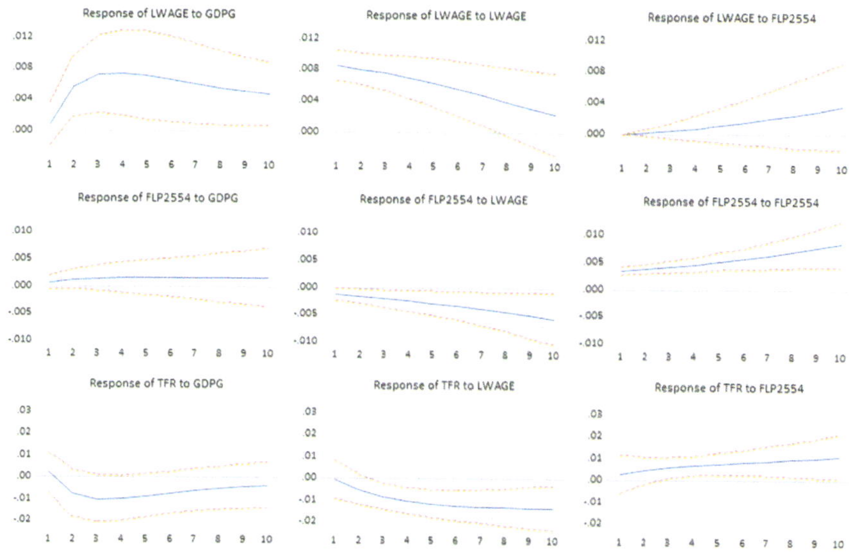

Fig. 1.4 Impulse response function by VAR model (selected figures)

$$\begin{array}{c} \text{TFR} - 3.7844 \times \text{FLP2554} + 1.7544 \times \text{LWAGE} - 8.2165 = 0 \\ (0.721) \qquad\qquad\qquad (0.2198) \\ \text{(Standard errors are in parentheses)} \end{array} \tag{1.8}$$

The element of loading matrix $\boldsymbol{\alpha}$ in TFR equation of error correction term is −0.3362, and the standard error is 0.0966, statistically significant, which means that the convergence time from temporary deviation to equilibrium is about 3 years. Note, GDPG is stationary series and exogeneous, so we should except it from ECM equation and it is dealt as exogeneous variable. Compared to simple VAR estimation result, the coefficient of FLP2554 is positive and of LWAGE is negative, and both are statistically significant, so almost the same results are obtained.

Figure 1.5 shows selected impulse response function results. The shock to LWAGE negatively affects TFR explicitly, and this shock is also negative to FLP2554. From these observations, increasing female wage works as opportunity cost for having a child to women, but this does not become incentive to increase labor provision. In addition, the shock to FLP2554 affects TFR positively as ECM estimation result described the above.

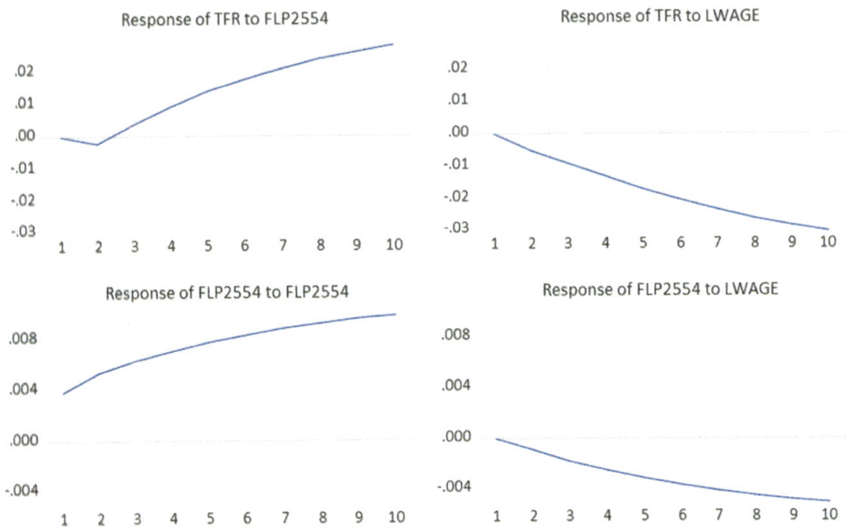

Fig. 1.5 Impulse response in ECM (selected figures)

1.5.3 Bayesian VAR Model

To estimate BVAR model, the optimal lag length should be determined by various information indicators. In this four-variable case, AIC, SC, and HQ criterion suggested that lag3 is the most recommended as Table 1.4 shows.

Before calculating BVAR model, it is necessary to determine hyper-parameter in prior distribution and standard deviation of $\boldsymbol{\theta}$, that is, given $\widehat{\sum}_{\varepsilon}$. Hyper-parameter, $\lambda_1, \lambda_2, \lambda_3$, means an importance of prior, a strongness with other dependent variables, and a degree of decay of own lagged variable, in turn. From Koop and Korobilis (2010), we set $\lambda_1 = 0.01$, $\lambda_2 = 0.99$, and $\lambda_3 = 1$; furthermore $\theta_0 = 0$. In addition, $\widehat{\sum}_{\varepsilon}$ is obtained from standard deviation of univariate OLS estimation result in

Table 1.4 Optimal lag length of BVAR

Lag	LogL	AIC	SC	HQ
0	161.930	−8.829	−8.697	−8.783
1	349.814	−18.767	−18.240*	−18.583
2	356.906	−18.661	−17.738	−18.339
3	373.917	−19.106*	−17.787	−18.646*
4	379.651*	−18.925	−17.210	−18.326

*indicates lag order selected by the criterion
AIC Akaike information criterion
SC Schwarz information criterion
HQ Hannan–Quinn information criterion

each equation. These assumptions of hyper-parameters are a standard setting in this section.

TFR equation in standard setting is

$$
\begin{aligned}
\text{TFR} = {} & \underset{(0.380)}{0.9500} \times \text{FLP2554}(-1) + \underset{(0.341)}{0.3190} \times \text{FLP2554}(-2) + \underset{(0.239)}{0.1876} \times \text{FLP2554}(-3) \\
& \underset{(0.178)}{-0.5837} \times \text{LWAGE}(-1) - \underset{(0.140)}{0.1463} \times \text{LWAGE}(-2) - \underset{(0.096)}{0.0898} \times \text{LWAGE} \\
& \underset{(0.080)}{+0.2515} \times \text{TFR}(-1) + \underset{(0.046)}{0.0442} \times \text{TFR}(-2) + \underset{(0.031)}{0.001} \times \text{TFR}(-3) + \underset{(0.588)}{4.3842}
\end{aligned}
\tag{1.9}
$$

and Table 1.5 shows estimation results of BVAR model in various settings as for hyper-parameter (Eq. (1.9) is the same as the second row of Table 1.5).

Figure 1.6 shows selected impulse response function results by BVAR model of standard settings. The shock to LWAGE negatively affects TFR, and this is same as the ECM result. Also, the shock to LWAGE on FLP2554 is negative; hence, this shock gives a negative effect; that is, increasing female wage relatively reduces female labor provision. In addition, the shock to FLP2554 positively affects TFR, which is also the same result that of in the ECM case.

In summary, both ECM and BVAR models suggest that increasing female wage works as opportunity cost for having a child to women, and female wage has dominant and fundamental effect to TFR or labor supply in Japan.

1.6 Government Policy and TFR

1.6.1 Government Policies and TFR

Family policies pertaining to instruments that provide support to young parents in-cash or in-kind might influence the decision of having children. Both affect the cost of children: In-cash provision explicitly helps budgetary condition of young families, while in-kind provision, such as providing nursery homes or support for expanding childcare leave, enables young families to combine working and rearing children.

Although analyzing the effects of government policies on TFR has been studied by numerous researchers, D'Addio and D'Ercole (2005) is one of the most widely recognized researches on this topic. They divided policies under three categories, namely tax benefits and cash transfers, childcare provision, and maternity and parental leaves. They estimated dynamic panel data using data from 16 OECD countries and concluded that higher transfers from government reduce the cost of children and raised TFR. Angela and Thévenon (2011) also confirmed that each policy package (paid leave, childcare services, and financial transfers) has a positive influence on TFR. On the other hand, Gauthier (2007) reviewed numerous studies and concluded that these studies reported small positive effect of government policies on TFR. Thus,

Table 1.5 Comparison of estimated results

Model	Dependent variable: TFR								
	Prior	Initial covariance	$\lambda 3$	LWAGE (−1)	LWAGE (−2)	LWAGE (−3)	FLP (−1)	FLP (−2)	FLP (−3)
VAR				−0.5298	0.3110	−0.5463	−0.6942	0.0760	2.2132
				(0.5277)	(0.8405)	(0.4675)	(1.2622)	(2.0347)	(1.5044)
BVAR	Litterman/Minnesota (1)	Univariate AR	1	−0.5837	−0.1463	−0.0898	0.9500	0.3190	0.1876
				(0.1783)	(0.1402)	(0.0963)	(0.3803)	(0.3412)	(0.2389)
BVAR	Litterman/Minnesota (2)	Full VAR	1	−0.6134	−0.1258	−0.0771	0.8436	0.3747	0.2464
				(0.1695)	(0.1352)	(0.0925)	(0.3878)	(0.3632)	(0.2546)
BVAR	Litterman/Minnesota (2)	Univariate AR	2	−0.7261	−0.0524	−0.0144	1.2020	0.0975	0.0237
				(0.1318)	(0.0760)	(0.0347)	(0.2870)	(0.1821)	(0.0826)
BVAR	Normal-Wishart			0.0069	0.0103	−0.0099	0.0169	0.0083	0.0039
				(0.6160)	(0.6958)	(0.5574)	(0.6222)	(0.7071)	(0.5911)

Note Hyper-parameters of Litterman/Minnesota: $\lambda 1 = 0.1$, $\lambda 2 = 0.99$, $\theta 0 = 0$, and of Normal-Wishart: $\lambda 1 = 0.1$, $\theta 0 = 0$
Lag length is 3, determined by AIC and HQ criterion
Values in parentheses are standard errors

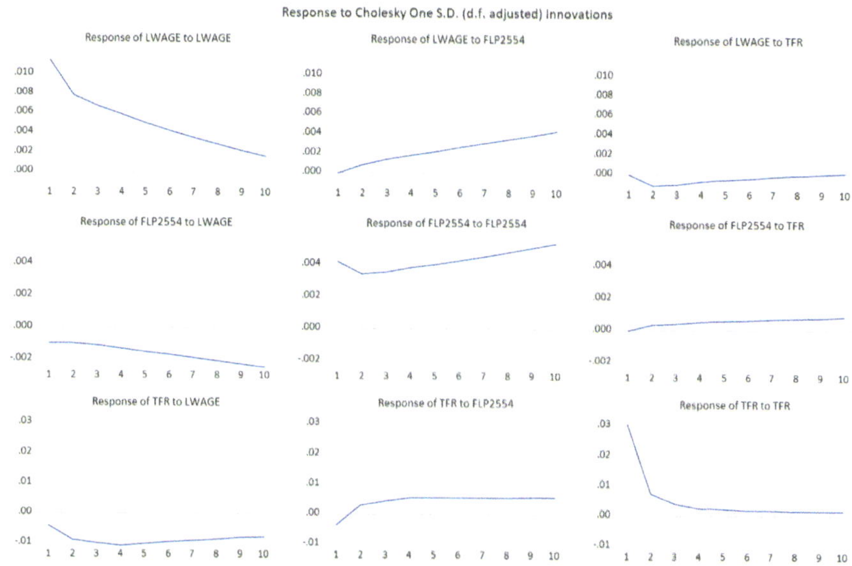

Fig. 1.6 Impulse response in BVAR

it may appear rather difficult to judge the effectiveness of government policies on TFR.

In this section, we consider that whether the government policy can improve TFR by benefitting social expenditure for young families. In order to confirm the effect of government policy, using the impulse response function of BVAR is appropriate tool.

1.6.2 Data and ECM Result

As variable of government expenditure, we chose social benefit to young families, which is named FAMILY in this study, and FAMILY is the ratio of public spending on young family, including child allowance, in-kind support for childcare or other spending, to the GDP. This public spending on young family is defined by the OECD "social expenditure."

FAMILY variable can be obtained from 1980 to 2017, and the data source is from "The Financial Statistics of Social Security in Japan" by National Institute of Population and Social Security Research. In short, although the value of FAMILY in 1980 was only 0.465% to GDP, the most recent value of that was 1.58% to GDP.

Before showing the BVAR model analysis, we confirmed cointegration and estimated ECM. Table 1.5 shows the results of the cointegration tests for (TFR, FLP2554, LWAGE, FAMILY) using Johansen's method. As same as previous section,

Table 1.6 Result of Johansen cointegration test

No. of Co	Eigenvalue	Trace statistics	Probability	Max eigen. stat	Probability
Variable: *TFR, FLP2554, LWAGE, FAMILY*					
r = 0*	0.6002	82.8090	0.0006	33.0067	0.0388
r = 1*	0.4876	49.8023	0.0089	24.0718	0.0837
r = 1	0.4017	25.7305	0.0521	18.4907	0.0671
r = 2	0.1822	7.2399	0.3201	7.2399	0.3201

Note * denotes rejection of the hypothesis at the 0.05 level
Lag interval (in first difference):1 to 1

we excluded GDPG in VECM setting. From Table 1.6, both trace test and max-eigenvalue test results reject null hypothesis of no cointegration at 1% statistically significance. Hence, it can estimate VECM model of four variables.

The error correction term of VECM is

$$\begin{array}{l}\text{TFR} + 1.3918 \times \text{FLP2554} + 0.7259 \times \text{LWAGEGAP} - 0.4500 \times \text{FAMILY} - 5.9430 = 0 \\ \qquad\qquad (1.582) \qquad\qquad (0.3102) \qquad\qquad (0.1083) \\ \qquad\qquad \text{(Standard errors are in parentheses)}\end{array} \tag{1.10}$$

The element of loading matrix $\boldsymbol{\alpha}$ in TFR equation of error correction term is −0.2933, and the standard error is 0.0708, statistically significant, which means that the convergence time from temporary deviation to equilibrium is about 3 years as almost same as previous VECM estimation. However, estimated coefficient of FLP2554 is negative to TFR and not statistically significant. In other words, it means that female labor provision has no effective influence to TFR.

1.6.3 Impulse Response of BVAR Model

In order to set the BVAR model, we confirmed the optimal lag length from some information criterions, and we adopted BVAR model with 1 lag.

Equation for TFR is as follows

$$\begin{array}{l}\text{TFR} = 0.4158 \times \text{TFR}(-1) + 0.7835 \times \text{FLP2554}(-1) - 0.6294 \times \text{LWAGE}(-1) \\ \qquad\qquad (0.0624) \qquad\qquad (0.3459) \qquad\qquad (0.0904) \\ -0.1394 \times \text{GDPG}(-1) + 0.0543 \times \text{FAMILY}(-1) + 3.6226 \\ \qquad\qquad (0.1086) \qquad\qquad (0.0249) \qquad\qquad (0.4089) \\ \text{(Standard errors are in parentheses)}\end{array} \tag{1.11}$$

Figure 1.7 shows selected impulse response function results by BVAR model with variable FAMILY.

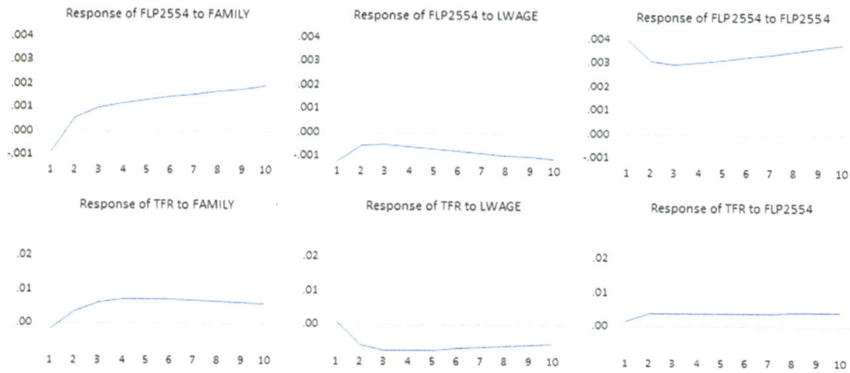

Fig. 1.7 Impulse response in BVAR with FAMILY (selected figures)

The shock to LWAGE negatively affects TFR, and this is same as the previous BVAR result. Also, the shock to LWAGE on FLP2554 is negative. In addition, the shock to FAMILY positively affects TFR, which means that the government policy of benefiting young family to improve TFR is appropriate. This point should be emphasized in this analysis.

1.7 Concluding Remarks and Policy Implications

Japan has been facing low fertility rate over the long period, and this low fertility situation is common in many developed and East Asian countries. Although there are so many studies that deal with low fertility from social and economic perspectives, it is difficult to find a research that points out the only cause of low fertility, because many factors affect the decision whether people will have a child or not.

This study explores the dynamic characteristics of the declining birth rate from a point of view of time series analysis. This study aimed to analyze the influences of labor participation and wage of women on fertility rate chiefly. In time series analysis, the number of data is limited and related variables are restricted. Therefore, it is more important to show the dynamic relationship between the relevant variables and the fertility rate than to specify the only cause of low fertility rate. There have been discussions whether there is a positive or negative relationship between female's labor force participation rate and fertility rate.

Generally, VAR model may be used to confirm the dynamic relationship among relevant variables; however, it is not easy to use because the variables have unit root. Therefore, in this study, we verified the dynamic relationship using ECM and BVAR model.

As a result, our models show that female's wage has a negative impact on fertility rate, and this is the same result obtained by both ECM and BVAR models. In other words, as many studies claimed, women's wages are an opportunity cost of having children, and we reconfirmed this fact in Japan's experience. In addition, this fact means that the compatible situation for women between labor provision and rearing children has been insufficient in Japan. In addition, including the government benefits to young family to BVAR model, then it was shown that this affects positively to TFR from the calculation of impulse response function. This can be interpreted that the government benefits reduce the opportunity cost of children; hence, the intervention by government in order to improve TFR is proper policy.

The purpose of this study was to explore factors of low fertility in Japan, and from the above empirical results, opportunity cost of children is the influential factor of low fertility rate. We also found the possibility that the government can improve fertility rate by some appropriate policies. There are many evidences (e.g., Luci-Greulich & Thévenon, 2013) that the governmental support by both in-cash and in-kind benefits from the government to the young household would support family formation. Low fertility will induce population decline in the future; thus, to prevent severe social upheaval caused by demographic change, the government should prepare proper family policies. This is not only for Japanese government, but also for many developed countries which are suffered from low birth rate.

In Japan, from the early 1990s, the government implemented various policies to improve fertility rate. Although the spending on such policies by the Japanese government is small compared with other European countries, the spending is gradually increasing. However, the volume and scale of benefits from the government to young families to rise TFR are not sufficient compared to European countries. On the other hand, our government is facing budgetary difficulties; that is, we have vast volume of public debt; hence, it is hard to increase spending in order to improve birth rate. We should solve this hard population problem for our descendants.

References

Ahn, N., & Mira, P. (2002). A note on the changing relationship between fertility and female employment rates in developed countries. *Journal of Population Economics, 15*, 667–682.

Angela, L., & Thévenon. O. (2011). *The impact of family policy packages on fertility trends in developed countries, hal-00657603.* https://hal.archives-ouvertes.fr/hal-00657603

Becker, G.S. (1960). An economic analysis of fertility. In A. Coale, (Ed.), *Universities-National Bureau Conference Series NO.11.* Princeton University Press.

Butz, W. P., & Ward, M. P. (1979). The emergence of counter cyclical U.S. fertility. *The American Economic Review, 69*, 318–328.

Cabinet Office. (2005). *Declining Birthrate White Paper 2005.* Cabinet Office. (in Japanese)

D'Addio, A., & D'Ercole, M. (2005). *Trends and determinants of fertility rates: the role of policies.* OECD Social Employment and Migration Working Papers, No. 27.

Engelhardt, H., Kőgel, T., & Prskawetz, A. (2004). Fertility and women's employment reconsidered: A macro-level time-series analysis for developed countries, 1900–2000. *Population Studies, 58*, 109–120.

Gauthier, A. (2007). The impact of family policies on fertility in industrialized countries: A review of the literature. *Population Research and Policy Review, 26*, 323–346.

Imai, H. (1996). Analysis of Japan's fertility using Butz-ward model. *Journal of Polution Problem, 52*(2), 30–35. National Institute of Population and Social Security Research (in Japanese).

Jaba, E., Chirianu, I., Balan, C., Robu, I.-B., & Roman, M. D. (2016). The analysis of the effect of women's participation in the labor market on fertility in European Union countries using welfare state models. *Economic Computation and Economic Cybernetics Studies and Research, 50*, 69–84.

Kato, H. (1997). Time series analysis of fertility change in Postwar Japan. *Journal of Population Studies (Jinkogaku Kenkyu), 20*, 23–34. Population Association of Japan.

Kato, H. (2020). Does a relationship between fertility and labor participation of women really exist? Perspectives from time series analysis. *International Journal of Economic Policy Studies, 14*(1), 1–21.

Kőgel, T. (2004). Did the association between fertility and female employment within OECD countries really change in sign? *Journal of Population Economics, 17*, 45–65.

Koop, G. M., & Korobilis, D. (2009). Bayesian multivariate time series methods for empirical macroeconomics. *Foundations and Trends® in Econometrics, 3*(4), 267–358.

Kuschnig, N., & Vashold, L. (2019). BVAR: Bayesian vector autoregressions with hierarchical prior selection in R. Department of Economics Working Paper Series, No. 296, WU Vienna University of Economics and Business.

Lee, H. Y. G., & Lee, S. P. (2014). Childcare availability, fertility and female labor force participation in Japan. *Journal of the Japanese and International Economies, 32*, 71–85.

Leibenstein, H. (1957). *Economic backwardness and economic growth.* Wiley.

Luci-Greulich, A., & Thévenon, O. (2013). The impact of family policies on fertility trends in developed countries. *European Journal of Population/revue Européenne De Démographie, 29*(4), 387–416.

Mincer, J. (1963). Market prices, opportunity costs, and income effects. In C. Christ, et al. (Eds.), *Measurement in economics: Studies in mathematical economics and econometrics in memory of Yehuda Grunfeld*. Stanford University Press.

Mishra, V., & Smyth, R. (2014). Female labor force participation and total fertility rates in the OECD: New evidence from panel cointegration and Granger causality testing. *Journal of Economics and Business, 62*, 48–64.

Ogawa, N., & Mason, A. (1986). An economic analysis of recent fertility in Japan: An application of the butz-ward model. *Journal of Population Studies (Jinkogaku Kenkyu), 9*, 5–14. Population Association of Japan.

Shastri, V. (2015). *The Changing relationship between fertility and female employment*. CMC Senior Theses. Paper 1094, http://scholarship.claremont.edu/cmc_theses/1094

Sims, C. A. (1980). Macroeconomics and reality. *Econometrica, 48*, 1–48.

Suzuki, S. (2018). *Structural changes in the patterns of Japanese fertility, discussion Pappr series, ERSS17-01*. Economic Research Society.

Toda, A.. (2007). *Empirical analysis of birth rate*. RIETI discussion paper series 07-J-007, Research Institute of Economy, Trade and Industry. (in Japanese)

Willis, R. J. (1973). A new approach to the economic theory of fertility behavior. *Journal of Political Economy, 81*(2), S14–S64.

Yamaguchi, K.. (2005). *The true relationship between female labor supply ad birth rate.* RIETI Discussion Paper Series 05-J-036, Research Institute of Economy, Trade and Industry. (in Japanese)

Chapter 2
Analysis of the Regional Disparity in the Total Fertility Rate in Japan—From the Perspective of Population Density and Socioeconomic Factors

Abstract This chapter examines the background of the disparity in the TFR at the municipality level. The large regional disparity in the TFR is driven by the differences in child-related costs, the work/life balance between employment and child-rearing for young families, the existence of a young population, and the policies of municipalities. Among these factors, we consider the relationship between the TFR and population density in particular. In economic studies of birth behavior, direct children-related and opportunity costs are important factors affecting the birth behavior of young families. Furthermore, those costs are heavily determined by the place of residence. It is often reported that the TFR is relatively low in municipalities with high population density. Urban areas with high population density are incompatible for young families raising children and working, and rarely provide nursery facilities. Additionally, the high housing cost generates suburbanization and leads to long-distance commuting. Hence, population density is a proxy variable for children-related costs. Additionally, the rate of female labor force participation is used as a proxy for an environment in which employment and child-rearing are compatible and flexible for female workers and young families. We also adopt the ratio of young women to the total population to represent the age structure in the municipality and variables such as child welfare expenses, nursery school capacity, and the number of children on the waiting list for nursery school to account for the municipality's fertility rate improvement policy. Using the TFR data in 2015, we examined the relationship between the TFR and socioeconomic variables. Furthermore, we prepared pooled data, including the TFR and socioeconomic variables, adding 2010 data to 2015 data. A three-period dataset including data in 2015, 2010, and 2005 is also used in the empirical analysis. We find that the coefficient of population density is negative and that of the female labor force participation rate is positive, and both are statistically significant. These findings suggest that children-related costs negatively influence the TFR and the compatible environment has a positive influence. Finally, a large young population and the government's policy for raising the TFR positively affect the TFR. In contrast, an increase in the number of children on the waiting list for nursery school negatively affects the TFR.

Keywords Total fertility rate · Population density · Female labor force participation · Children-related costs

H. Kato, *Macro-econometric Analysis on Determinants of Fertility Behavior*, Population Studies of Japan, https://doi.org/10.1007/978-981-16-3927-2_2

2.1 Introduction

The total fertility rate (TFR) in Japan has been declining since the mid-1970s, and it reached 1.26 in 2005, the lowest level since World War II. Although the TFR rose slightly thereafter, it was still just 1.32 in 2019, a low level from the perspective of the maintenance of the population size. While this situation is a national one, there are large regional disparities in the TFR. For example, Okinawa prefecture has the highest rate at 1.82, whereas the TFR of the Tokyo metropolitan area is only 1.24, a difference of 0.58 points. The regional disparity in the TFR by prefecture has narrowed in recent years compared with the past, but it remains large. Further, the regional disparity in the TFR at the municipality level is much larger than that in the prefectural level. Observing the estimated TFRs by municipality in 2015 (rates from 2013 to 2017), there is a difference of 1.63 points between 2.47 in Kin, Okinawa prefecture, and 0.84 in Toyono, Osaka prefecture.

This study analyzes the factors behind these disparities in the TFR. The large disparity in the TFR at the municipality level is driven by the differences in children-related costs, the work/life balance between employment and child-rearing for young families, the existence of a young population, and the policies of municipalities. Among these factors, we consider the relationship between the TFR and population density in particular. While many empirical studies have found the factors behind the disparities in the TFR by prefecture and municipality, few studies have dealt with the relationship between population density and the TFR. In this study, we treat population density as a proxy variable for children-related costs and analyze the relationship with the TFR. In addition, the relationship between other factors such as work/life balance and the policies of municipalities and the TFR is empirically examined in this study.

The remainder of this paper is organized as follows. Firstly, in Sect. 2.2, the recent statistics of the regional TFR are shown and we describe the characteristics of the municipality-level TFR. In Sect. 2.3, we summarize the related literature. More concretely, studies of the relation between population density and the birth rate and empirical analyses of the determinants of the TFR in Japan are introduced. In Sect. 2.4, we show the mechanism behind the disparity in the TFR in urban and rural areas using hypotheses and a simple theoretical model. In Sect. 2.5, the data used in this study are described and we summarize the descriptive statistics. Sections 2.6 and 2.7 provide the main empirical results. A dataset based on 1730 municipalities in 2015 is analyzed in Sect. 2.6, and a three-period dataset is used in Sect. 2.7. Lastly, concluding remarks are in Sect. 2.8.

2.2 TFR in Japan's Prefectures and Municipalities

As explained in the Introduction, although Japan's TFR rose from the lowest level after World War II in 2005, it has stagnated in the 2010s and it was just 1.32 in 2019.

On the contrary, there has been a disparity in the regional TFR in recent years. In this section, we describe the regional TFR.

2.2.1 Recent TFR in Prefectures

In 2019, the prefecture that had the highest TFR was Okinawa (1.82). The TFR in Okinawa has long been the highest among all prefectures in Japan. On the contrary, the Tokyo metropolitan area recorded the lowest TFR in 2019 (1.15). Since 1980, Tokyo's TFR has been the lowest of all prefectures. In 2019, the second highest TFR was 1.73 in Miyazaki, followed by 1.68 in Shimane and 1.66 in Nagasaki. On the contrary, the second lowest TFR was 1.23 in Miyagi, followed by 1.24 in Hokkaido and 1.25 in Kyoto. In general, the TFR in western prefectures in Japan is a little higher than that in eastern prefectures (i.e., prefectures located to the east of Mie prefecture). In 2019, the mean TFR in western prefectures was 1.52 compared with 1.39 in eastern prefectures.

We next discuss the TFR disparity in prefectures from 2000 to 2019 based on the maximum and minimum TFRs. In 1980, the TFR in Okinawa was 2.38 compared with 1.44 in Tokyo, a difference of 0.94. In 1990, the TFR in both prefectures declined (1.95 in Okinawa and 1.23 in Tokyo), meaning the difference reduced slightly to 0.72. In 2000, the TFR in Okinawa was 1.82 and that in Tokyo was 1.07, a difference of 0.75. As explained above, the difference in the TFR in 2019 was 0.67.

Figure 2.1 shows the trend of the national TFR and its standard deviation (SD) by prefecture from 2000 to 2019. The SD of the TFR in prefectures was 0.132 in 2000, which declined slightly to 0.120 in 2006 and increased to 0.139 in 2019. Interestingly,

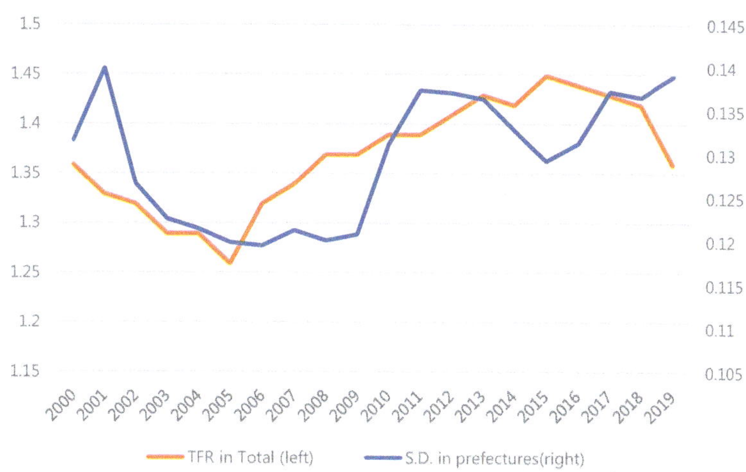

Fig. 2.1 Disparity of TFR in prefectures. *Data* Ministry of Health, Labour and Welfare "Vital Statistics"

the SD of the TFR in prefectures changed with the national TFR. As described in the Introduction, Japan's TFR recorded its lowest value in 2005, and the SD in prefectures started to increase from 2005. From Fig. 2.1, the SD in prefectures and national TFR seem to be correlated with each other, and the correlation coefficient is 0.593. In other words, raising the national TFR accompanies increasing disparity in the TFR in prefectures.

2.2.2 *TFR in Municipalities in 2015*

In this subsection, the origins of the data on the TFR in municipalities are introduced and we summarize the TFR in municipalities in 2015.

(1) Data

In general, it is difficult to calculate the TFR in small regions such as towns and villages because the probability of events such as births occurring is unstable as region size falls. Considering this difficulty, the Ministry of Health, Labour and Welfare publishes an estimated TFR by municipality in its Special Report from the Vital Statistics. Because of the instability of calculating the TFR in small regions, this Special Report from the Vital Statistics adopts a unique estimation. Firstly, the female birth rate in five-year age groups from 15 to 49 years in each municipality over five years including the Population Census year and the years before and after is estimated using the Bayesian method to calculate the TFR. In this study, we use TFR data from 2013 to 2017. The female population in each age group is based on the calculation of the birth rate from the 2015 Population Census published by the Statistics Bureau, the Ministry of Internal Affairs and Communications. The overview of the Bayes estimation method by the Special Report from the Vital Statistics is as follows:

(1) Collect data on the number of births and female population in five-year age groups in each municipality, and calculate the mean birth rate over these five years. In addition, calculate the number of births and female population in five-year age groups in the prefecture to which the municipality belongs.
(2) Using the female population in the five-year age groups in each municipality as a weight, obtain the weighted mean and variance of the birth rate in the five-year age groups in the prefecture to which the municipality belongs. From this mean birth rate of the prefecture, the estimated TFR in the prefecture can be obtained by multiplying the above birth rate by 5.
(3) Using the weighted mean birth rate in the prefecture from (2), calculate the estimated TFR using the Bayesian method. Assuming that the birth rate of the five-year age groups calculated above follows a beta distribution, obtain the parameters of the beta distribution from the weighted mean and variance of the birth rate in the prefecture. If these parameters are α and β, the beta distribution is described as $Be(\alpha, \beta)$ and the expected value is $\alpha/(\alpha + \beta)$. This is the prior distribution of the Bayesian estimation.

(4) Lastly, based on the concept of Bayesian updating, using the birth rate (r) and population (n) in the five-year age groups in each municipality derived from (1), the estimated birth rate (b) can be calculated using the Bayesian method as $b = (\alpha + r)/(\alpha + \beta + n)$, and we can estimate the TFR of each municipality. From here, we treat the estimated TFR for 2013 to 2017, which is calculated using the Bayesian method as the TFR for 2015.

(2) Distribution of the Municipality-level TFR in 2015

Figure 2.2 shows the distribution of the TFR of 1730 municipalities (including the 23 wards of the Tokyo metropolitan area and the ordinance-designated city's TFR for the entire area) in 2015 from the Special Report from the Vital Statistics. This figure also shows the descriptive statistics of the TFR over these 1730 municipalities, where the mean is 1.519 and median is 1.507. This mean value is somewhat higher than the nationwide TFR, which is 1.45 in 2015. This difference is caused by the low TFR in urban areas, which have a larger population than rural areas. In addition, the variance of the 1730 municipalities is 0.041 and the SD is 0.202.

As stated in the Introduction, the highest TFR of all the 1730 municipalities is 2.47 at Kin in Okinawa prefecture. The next highest TFRs are 2.46 at Isen in Kagoshima prefecture, 2.40 at Tokunoshima in Kagoshima prefecture, and 2.35 at Miyakojima-shi in Okinawa prefecture. The TFRs in the municipalities that belong to the islands of Kagoshima and Okinawa prefectures are relatively high. On the contrary, among the 1730 municipalities, the lowest TFR is 0.84 at Toyono in Osaka prefecture, followed by 0.94 at Toshima Ward in the Tokyo metropolitan area, 0.96 at Tobetsu in Hokkaido, and 0.97 at Moroyama in Saitama prefecture.

(3) Comparison with the TFRs in 2010 and 2015

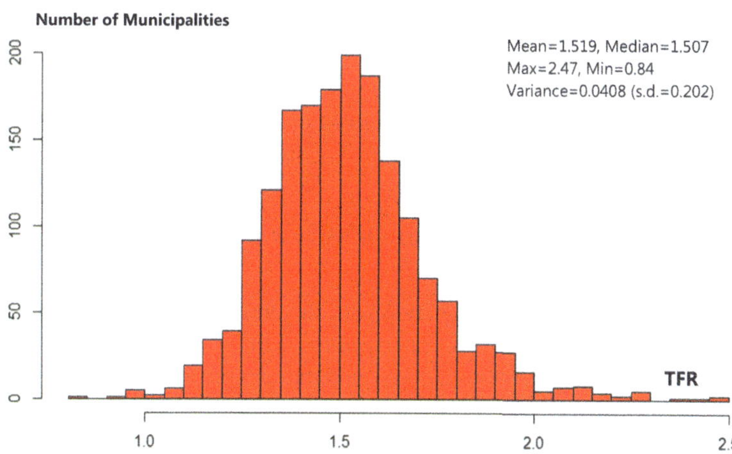

Fig. 2.2 Histogram of dispersion of TFR in 2015. *Data* The Ministry of Health, Labour and Welfare (2020), "Vital Statistics in Japan, Special Report"

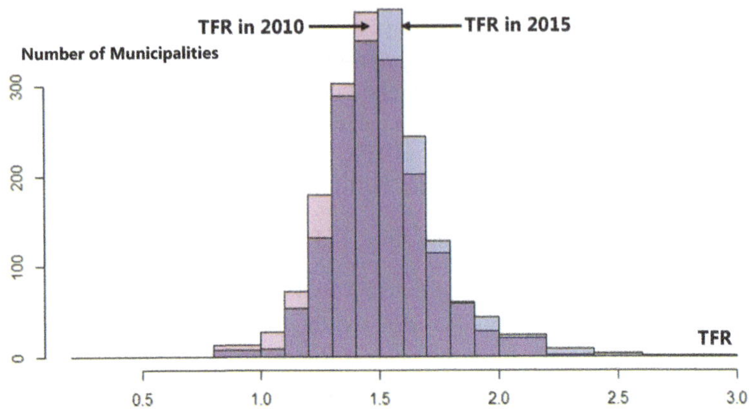

Fig. 2.3 TFR comparison in 2015 and in 2010. Data: The Ministry of Health, Labour and Welfare (2015, 2020), "Vital Statistics in Japan, Special Report"

The TFR by municipality in 2008–2012 (2010 data hereafter) has also been published, and Kato (2018) analyzed the TFR distribution using these data. In this study, the municipalities as of 2010 are adjusted to match the data as of 2015, and the TFRs of the 1730 municipalities are obtained. Using this dataset, we compare the distribution of the municipality-level TFRs in 2010 and 2015. Figure 2.3 shows an overlay of the histograms of the TFR at these two time points. In the 2010 data, the mean TFR is 1.487, which is lower than the mean value in 2015; hence, the histogram of 2015 is slightly shifted to the right. For reference, the variance in the 2010 data is 0.0412, similar to that in the 2015 data.

2.3 Related Literature

In this section, previous empirical analyses of the TFR are summarized.

2.3.1 Literature on Population Density and Birth Rates

Although studies of the relation between birth rates and population density are limited, some provide an interesting perspective. Lutz and Qiang (2002) surveyed empirical studies of the relation between population density and birth rates at the country level and found evidence of a negative correlation between them. However, they summarized that few systematic and theoretical attempts have been made to consider fertility and population. Lutz and Qiang (2002) included population density as an indicator of urbanization and confirmed the negative relationship between it and the fertility rate using data from 187 countries from 1960 to 1990. Lutz et al.

(2006) extended the finding of the negative relationship between population density and the reproduction rate to biology, finding that this relation is common in animals in general. They estimated this relationship in 145 countries including developing countries using panel data from 1960 to 2000 and confirmed the significant negative effect of population density on the fertility rate. Tang and Chen (2002) also analyzed birth rates and population density.

Croix and Gobbi (2015) investigated the relation between fertility and population density with reference to Malthus' population theory, finding that agricultural income in areas of high population density is low and that people in those areas often delay marriage as a result; they also discussed whether this drives the negative relation between fertility and population density. They stated that modern thinking suggests that income is high in areas that exit the agglomeration economy and that the birth rate is low in high-income areas, meaning that a negative relation is observed between fertility and income. In addition, they discussed whether people who have a relatively weak (strong) preference for children live in urban (rural) areas, which could again drive the negative relation between fertility and population density. Croix and Gobbi (2017) later found that fertility rates are negatively affected by population density using micro data on 44 developing countries. They calculated that a rise in density from 10 to 1000 inhabitants per square kilometer corresponds to a decrease in fertility of about 0.7 children.

Sato (2007) aimed to verify the relation between fertility and population movement by introducing the agglomeration economy and congestion in urban areas using a two-period overlapping generation model. This theoretical interpretation was that the agglomeration economy influences the birth rate from both an income and a substitution effect; the former has a positive effect, and the latter has a negative effect. He also estimated the negative relationship between fertility and population density by considering the effect of the agglomeration economy using data from 47 Japanese prefectures in 2000.

Alvarez Diaz et al. (2018) analyzed empirically the relation between population growth and population density in EU subregions, concluding that population density has a negative correlation with population growth. In their study, population growth included population migration, not only reproduction; however, they found that population density is a crucial factor in population dynamics. In many of the studies examining the socioeconomic factors that determine the TFR, such as Lutz and Qiang (2002) and Alvarez Diaz et al. (2018), population density is used as an indicator of urbanization. However, few studies consider population density as a proxy of children-related costs. The perspective that population density is accompanied by children-related costs is one viewpoint of our study.

2.3.2 Empirical Analysis of the Determinants of the TFR in Japan

Considerable research has examined the socioeconomic factors that affect birth behavior in Japan, including studies by academic researchers as well as reports by governments and private-sector think tanks. Studies analyze the regional socioeconomic characteristics that affect the TFR using various methods. For prefectural-level analysis, Unayama and Yamamoto (2015), Tanabe and Suzuki (2016), and Adachi and Nakazato (2017) are representative studies, who estimated the factors that affect birth behavior. On the contrary, Kamata and Iwasawa (2009), Abe and Harada (2008), and Kato (2018) analyzed municipality-level data.

Unayama and Yamamoto (2015) measured the effectiveness of nursery school provision on the TFR and female labor force participation rate using panel data at the prefecture level from 1996 to 2012. They used cohort data converted from time series data. In their study, potential nursery school capacity has a significant positive effect on the TFR. Their estimation results show that if potential nursery school capacity increases by 1%, the TFR increases by 0.02–0.03. Tanabe and Suzuki (2016) analyzed the relationship between the TFR and 68 socioeconomic variables such as housing, income, medical care, welfare, and education in 47 prefectures using the support vector machine methodology, a type of nonlinear regression analysis. Tanabe and Suzuki (2016) confirmed that the marriage rate, male unemployment rate, and percentage of women in managerial positions have significant effects on the TFR. In addition, Adachi and Nakazato (2017) empirically analyzed the determinants of the TFR in prefectures using annual data from 1985 to 2010. Combining original data with cohort data, they found that increases in the unmarried rate and in female wages have a significant negative effect on the TFR. These findings suggest that the opportunity cost of marriage and child-rearing is an important factor regarding birth behavior.

Kamata and Iwasawa (2009) focused on regional differences in the TFR in 2311 municipalities in 2005 from the viewpoint of the spatial effect on fertility behavior. Using geographically weighted regression, they considered the geographical heterogeneity in the estimated regression equations. According to their estimation results, the ratios of university graduates and unmarried women have a negative effect on the TFR, whereas the number of nursery schools has a positive effect. Abe and Harada (2008) carried out a cross-sectional regression using data on 3234 municipalities in 2000. They concluded that the high income and high cost of women's time, as the opportunity cost of child-rearing, and high housing costs represented by land prices negatively impact the TFR. Nishimoto and Suruga (2011) examined the relationship between the TFR and socioeconomic variables using 638 municipalities in 2000. They clarified that the higher the nursery school fees, the lower is the birth rate and that three generations living together have a positive effect on the TFR.

Kato (2018) focused on the relationship between population density and the TFR as in this study; however, we revise the data and re-estimate the socioeconomic factors that affect the TFR at the municipality level as well as compare the results with those of previous estimations. Kato (2018) found a negative relationship between population density and the TFR and a positive relationship between the female labor force participation rate and the TFR.

2.4 Population Density and Birth Behavior

Many studies have shown that children-related costs are an important factor in determining birth behavior and population density could serve as a proxy indicator. In this section, this discussion is summarized.

2.4.1 *Population Density as a Proxy Variable of Children-Related Costs*

In economics studies of birth behavior, both the direct children-related costs and opportunity costs are important factors that affect the birth behavior of young families. Furthermore, those costs are heavily determined by place of residence. Labor and capital are concentrated in urban areas as opposed to rural areas, meaning that urban areas have higher efficiency and productivity, which leads to higher incomes. These situations are identified as agglomeration economies. Hence, population density can be understood as the degree of agglomeration. On the contrary, areas with higher population density have a higher land price or rent and higher housing costs for young families. In addition, higher land prices constrain the space in residential areas, which could limit the number of children that a young family has in the future.

Urban areas with high population density are incompatible with child-rearing and female labor force participation. More concretely, high residential costs generate suburbanization and lead to long-distance commuting. Hence, it is necessary to use the land in urban areas more effectively. As a result, there is a shortage of nursery resources and parks for children in urban areas. From the above discussions, higher population density has a negative effect on the decision to have children. Taken together, population density may influence birth behavior.

2.4.2 *Model of Population Density and Birth Behavior*

Although many empirical studies treat population density as a proxy variable of urbanization, few discuss the relation between fertility and population density theoretically. Here, we confirm the relation between population density and the fertility rate from the microeconomic perspective. The following model is modified from that of Croix and Gobbi (2016) to suit the purpose of our study.

Firstly, we assume that an individual obtains utility from consuming and having children. For simplicity, we consider only the number of children and ignore their quality. In addition, income is spent on the consumption of general goods and children-related costs; then, the optimal problem for a rational individual is

$$\begin{aligned} \max \quad & u = \ln(c) + \gamma \ln(n) \\ \text{s.t.} \quad & y = c + \delta n \end{aligned} \tag{2.1}$$

In the above problem, c is consumption per capita, n is the number of children, y is income per capita, γ measures the preference for children, and δ is the child-rearing cost for one child. δ can be expressed as a function of per capita income and population density:

$$\delta = \lambda P^{\alpha} y \tag{2.2}$$

Areas that have high population density P show high land prices; hence, the cost of supplying child-rearing resources and housing costs (rent or living space) are higher than in areas with low population density. λ is a parameter that connects population density and income/child-rearing cost, which is constant in all areas.

Comparing the child-rearing cost in two areas, U and R, where U means urban areas and R means rural areas, from Eq. (2.2), we obtain

$\frac{\delta_U}{\delta_R} = \left(\frac{P_U}{P_R}\right)^{\alpha} \frac{y_U}{y_R}$.

If we assume $\frac{P_U}{P_R} > 1$, then $\frac{\delta_U}{\delta_R} > \frac{y_U}{y_R}$ is derived.

Next, solving the simple static optimal problem described Eq. (2.1), and demand for children is

$$n^* = \frac{\gamma}{\delta(1+\gamma)} y \tag{2.3}$$

Demand for children in urban areas is n_U and that in rural areas is n_R:

$$n_R^* - n_U^* = \frac{\gamma}{1+\gamma}\left[\frac{y_R}{\delta_R} - \frac{y_U}{\delta_U}\right]$$

Furthermore, $\frac{\delta_U}{\delta_R} > \frac{y_U}{y_R}$ is satisfied; hence,

$$n_R^* > n_U^* \tag{2.4}$$

From the above, the claim that optimal demand for children in rural areas is more than that in urban areas is confirmed. Hence, an individual who lives in a high population density area has lower demand for children, meaning a negative relation between the TFR and population density, as discussed above.

2.4.3 *Other Factors that Affect the TFR*

The TFR is influenced not only by population density and children-related costs but also by other socioeconomic factors. Three factors are introduced into the empirical analysis below. Firstly, we include the female labor force participation rate. Many empirical studies find a positive correlation between female labor force participation and the TFR using prefecture-level data. This suggests that if female workers have better employment conditions, they could obtain a compatible and flexible environment for child-rearing and work. From this view, we should consider the supply of female labor as a proxy variable for an environment in which employment and child-rearing are compatible for women and young families.

Secondly, variables in concern with improving environment for child-rearing environment should be discussed. Since the 1990s, the government has formulated policies to raise the low fertility rate, including improving the child-rearing environment by, for example, providing nursery schools and increasing government expenditure for children. Although the childcare environment has been improved by these policies, many children remain on waiting lists for nursery school in urban municipalities. Thus, it is important to verify whether the differences in childcare policies by municipality affect the disparities in the TFR.

Thirdly, the existence of a young population is a necessary condition in municipalities that have a high TFR. In addition, marriage is an important precondition for young families to have a child in Japan, meaning that variables related to the young population and marriage are also necessary. The ratios of unmarried women and young women are other important variables. Other factors may further influence the TFR, as we show in the estimation results.

2.5 Data and Descriptive Statistics

2.5.1 *Data Source*

To analyze the TFR, we select variables that might affect birth behavior following the above discussion: population density, the female labor force participation rate, nursery school capacity, the ratio of child welfare expenses to general tax revenue, the number of children on a waiting list for nursery school (termed "number of waiting children" hereafter), the ratio of the population of women aged 18–39 years to the total population, the net migration rate, the ratio of primary industry employment, the percentage of unmarried women, and taxable income. The data source and characteristics of the TFR were explained in the previous section. We obtain those data from 1730 municipalities in 2015; hence, the number of samples in the basic regression analysis is 1730.

The data on population density, the female labor force participation rate, the ratio of the population of women aged 18–39 years to the total population, the ratio of primary industry employment, and the percentage of unmarried women are from the Population Census published by the Statistics Bureau. The female labor force participation rate is calculated as the total female labor force divided by the female population aged 15–64 years. The ratio of primary industry employment is obtained as the number of people employed in the primary industry divided by the total number of employed people in the municipality.

Nursery school capacity is measured as the maximum capacity of a nursery school in the municipality divided by the population aged 0–5 years in the same municipality. The data on nursery school capacity are from the "Survey on Social Welfare Facilities" published by the Ministry of Health, Labour and Welfare, and those on the population aged 0–5 years are from the Population Census published by the Statistics Bureau. The ratio of child welfare expenses is the ratio of expenditure on child welfare to general tax revenue in the municipality. Because general expenditure is an indicator that does not specify its purpose of usage, this ratio shows the weight of the policy direction on raising the TFR and supporting children in the municipality. The data on the ratio of child welfare expenses are obtained from the "Local Financial Situation Survey" published by the Statistics Bureau. The data on the number of waiting children are from the "Survey on the Number of Waiting Children" published by the Ministry of Health, Labour and Welfare. The net migration rate is calculated as the number of net immigrants divided by the total population in the municipality; these data are obtained from the "Report on Internal Migration in Japan" published by the Statistics Bureau. Lastly, taxable income is from the "Report of Municipal Taxation Status" published by the Ministry of Internal Affairs and Communications.

2.5.2 Descriptive Statistics

Tables 2.1 and 2.2 show the descriptive statistics of the variables. For population density, the mean is 1390.7 people per km^2 and the median is 500.8 people per km^2. Therefore, the two statistics show a large difference. The mean female labor force participation rate is 80.7%, and the median is 80.2%. Note that the female labor force participation rate is the total female labor force population divided by the female population aged 15–64 years, meaning that the rate may be over one in municipalities with many elderly workers. The maximum net migration rate is 3.9%, and the minimum is −5.8%.

For those variables related to the policy to raise the TFR, mean nursery school capacity is 0.483; however, the disparity in this variable is large (maximum 124.8% and minimum 0.0%). The mean ratio of child welfare expenses to the total budget is 19.2%. The minimum ratio of it is only 0.8% (Otoineppu-mura, the smallest municipality in Hokkaido), whereas the maximum ratio of it is 108.5% (Arakawa-ku, Tokyo). To confirm the absence of the multi-collinearity problem, the correlation matrix of the variables is shown.

Table 2.1 Basic statistics of 2015 data

	Average	Median	Max	Min	SD
TFR	1.519	1.507	2.470	0.838	0.202
Population density (logarithm)	1390.7	500.8	22,380.2	10.5	2564.5
Female labor participation rate	0.807	0.802	1.575	0.478	0.112
Capacity of nursery school	0.483	0.474	1.248	0.000	0.212
Ratio of child welfare expense to general tax revenue	0.192	0.184	1.085	0.008	0.112
Number of waiting children to nursery school	12.4	0.0	1109.0	0.0	54.5
Ratio of population of female 18–39 year old to total population	0.099	0.098	0.184	0.033	0.024
Net migration rate	−0.004	−0.004	0.039	−0.058	0.007
Ratio of primary industry employment	0.110	0.079	0.770	0.000	0.103
Percentage of unmarried female	23.8	23.7	45.3	13.0	3.8
Taxable income (logarithm)	298.3	2708.1	10,232.2	1984.3	524.4

Note The number of sample is 1730

2.6 Empirical Analysis 1: Basic Regression Results

2.6.1 Relations Among the Major Variables

Firstly, the relations among some of the major variables are confirmed (i.e., the TFR, population density, and female labor force participation rate). From the above discussion, a negative correlation is expected between the TFR and population density. Figure 2.4 shows a scatterplot of the TFR and population density. We regress the TFR on the logarithm of population density and find that population density has a negative coefficient (statistically significant). Figure 2.5 shows a scatterplot of the TFR and female labor force participation rate, highlighting the positive and statistically significant coefficient of female labor force participation. However, the scatterplot in Fig. 2.5 shows some heteroskedasticity, which is confirmed using White test and Breusch–Pagan–Godfrey test. Hence, hereafter, we show the standard errors of the estimated coefficients as White–Huber robust standard errors.

2.6.2 Basic Regression Result

Table 2.3 shows basic regression results for various combinations of the independent variables. The independent variables in Case (1) in Table 2.3 are population density, female labor force participation, nursery school capacity, and child welfare expenses. The coefficient of population density is -0.035, that of female labor force participation is 0.302, and that of child welfare expenses is 0.516, which are all statistically

Ta le 2.2 Correlation matrix of Basic statistics of 2015 data

	(1)	(2)	(3)	(4)	(5)	(6)	(7)	(3)	(9)	(10)	(11)
1. TFR	1	−0.141	0.1593	0.1191	−0.002	−0.121	−0.032	0.0179	0.1773	−0.242	−0.246
2. Population denslty (Logarlthm)		1	−0.722	−0.234	0.7703	0.334	0.7255	0.4662	−0.756	0.6309	0.6066
3. Female labor participation pate			1	0.4447	−0.622	−0.31	−0.731	−0.3B73	0.7154	−0.695	−0.603
4. Capacity of nursery school				1	−0.166	−0.172	−0.337	−0.186	0.295B	-0.35	−0.441
5. Ratio of child welfare expense to general tax revenue					1	0.435	0.7605	0.4775	−0.553	0.644	0.521
6. Number of waiting children to nursery school						1	0.3753	0.2259	−0.204	0.3396	0.3622
7. ratio of population of female 18–39 year old to total population							1	0.5541	−0.592	0.7936	0.6375
10. Net migration rate								1	−0.362	0.4063	0.4212
11. Ratio of primary industry employment									1	−0.562	−0.451
12. Percentage of unmarried female										1	0.5949
11.Taxable income (Logarithm)											1

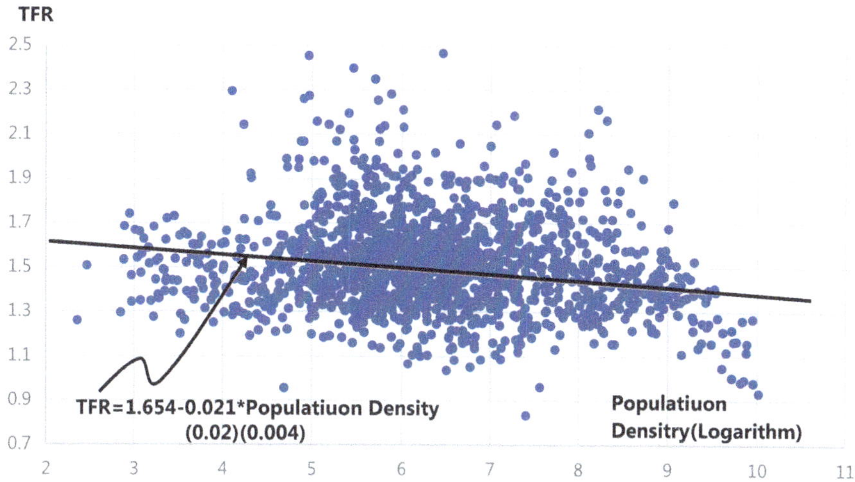

Fig. 2.4 TFR and population density. *Data* The Ministry of Health, Labour and Welfare, "Vital Statistics in Japan, Special Report," Statistics Bureau, "Population Census." *Note* White-Huber robust standard error in parentheses

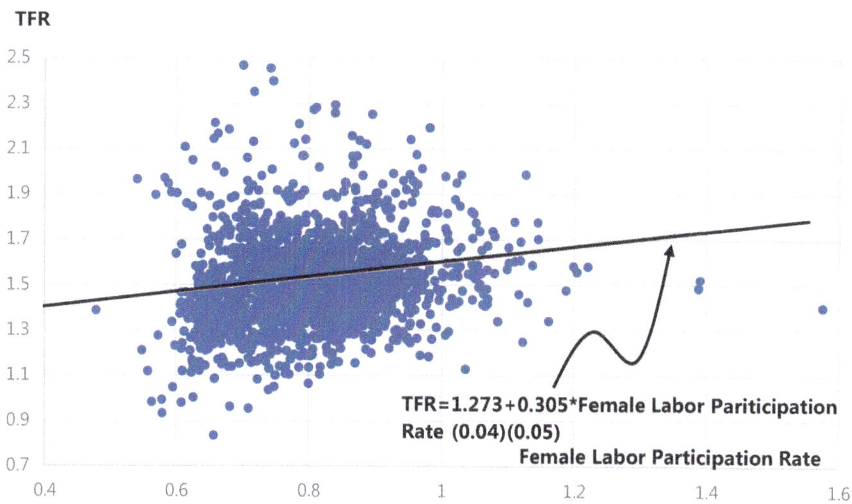

Fig. 2.5 TFR and female labor participation rate. *Data* The Ministry of Health, Labour and Welfare, "Vital Statistics in Japan, Special Report," Statistics Bureau, "Population Census," *Note* White-Huber robust standard error in parentheses

significant. However, the coefficient of nursery school capacity is not statistically significant. Case (2) excludes nursery school capacity and child welfare expenses from Case (1) and includes the ratio of the population of women aged 18–39 years. The coefficient of the ratio of the population of women aged 18–39 years is 1.108

Table 2.3 Estimation results for municipalities in 2015

	(1)	(2)	(3)	(4)	(5)	(6)	(7)	(8)	(9)	(10)	(11)	(12)
Const	1.388***	1.212***	1.220***	1.380***	1.185***	1.352***	1.260***	1.268***	1.249***	1.653***	1.791***	4.622***
	(0.085)	(0.108)	(0.107)	(0.108)	(0.108)	(0.107)	(0.112)	(0.112)	(0.110)	(0.112)	(0.109)	(0.466)
Population density (logarithm)	−0.035***	-0.014**	−0.016***	−0.036***	−0.013**	−0.034***	−0.013**	−0.015***	−0.003	−0.007	−0.027***	−0.017**
	(0.007)	(0.006)	(0.006)	(0.007)	(0.006)	(0.007)	(0.006)	(0.006)	(0.006)	(0.006)	(0.007)	(0.007)
Female labor participation rate	0.302***	0.355***	0.303***	0.306***	0.309***	0.315***	0.339***	0.291***	0.192**	0.160*	0.180**	0.101
	(0.077)	(0.082)	(0.086)	(0.082)	(0.086)	(0.082)	(0.083)	(0.087)	(0.093)	(0.082)	(0.074)	(0.074)
Capacity of nursery school	0.024	–	0.067**	0.025	0.064**	0.015	–	0.063**	0.062**	0.058**	–	–
	(0.027)	–	(0.027)	(0.029)	(0.027)	(0.028)	–	(0.028)	(0.027)	(0.027)	–	–
Ratio of child welfare expense to general tax revenue	0.516***	–	–	0.510***	–	0.586***	–	–	–	–	0.554***	0.457***
	(0.107)	–	–	(0.126)	–	(0.122)	–	–	–	–	(0.106)	(0.096)
Number of waiting children to nursery school	–	–	–	–	−0.0003***	−0.0005***	−0.0003***	−0.0003***	−0.0004***	−0.0002**	−0.0003***	−0.0002**
	–	–	–	–	(0.0001)	(0.0001)	(0.0001)	(0.0001)	(0.0001)	(0.0001)	(0.0001)	(0.0001)
Ratio of population of female 18–39 years old to total population	–	1.108***	1.229***	0.067	1.380***	0.117	0.853**	0.966**	0.895**	3.041***	1.814***	2.969***
	–	(0.369)	(0.369)	(0.436)	(0.366)	(0.425)	(0.349)	(0.381)	(0.378)	(0.437)	(0.476)	(0.481)
Net migration rate	–	–	–	–	–	–	2.703***	2.672***	2.711***	1.942**	1.687*	2.126**

(continued)

Table 2.3 (continued)

	(1)	(2)	(3)	(4)	(5)	(6)	(7)	(8)	(9)	(10)	(11)	(12)
	–	–	–	–	–	–	(0.924)	(0.920)	(0.898)	(0.914)	(0.881)	(0.879)
Ratio of primary industry employment	–	–	–	–	–	–	–	–	0.283***	–	–	–
	–	–	–	–	–	–	–	–	(0.085)	–	–	–
Percentage of unmarried female	–	–	–	–	–	–	–	–	–	−0.023***	-0.022***	-0.022***
	–	–	–	–	–	–	–	–	–	(0.003)	(0.003)	(0.003)
Taxable income	–	–	–	–	–	–	–	–	–	–	–	-0.369***
	–	–	–	–	–	–	–	–	–	–	–	(0.059)
Adjusted R^2	0.062	0.034	0.038	0.061	0.043	0.073	0.046	0.049	0.056	0.106	0.132	0.170
F value	29.47	21.51	17.93	23.57	16.58	23.72	17.67	15.79	15.57	30.17	38.50	45.15
Number of Sample	1730	1730	1730	1730	1730	1730	1730	1730	1730	1730	1730	1730

Note: Explained variable is TFR. White-Huber robust standard error in parentheses
In the table, *** means 1% significant, **means 5% significant, and * means 10% significant

(statistically significant). Furthermore, Case (3) adds nursery school capacity; its coefficient is 0.067, and it is statistically significant.

Case (6) has six independent variables. The estimated coefficients of population density, female labor force participation, child welfare expenses, and the number of waiting children are statistically significant (adjusted $R^2 = 0.073$). These results confirm that population density has a negative relation with the TFR, whereas female labor force participation and the variables related to the policy to raise the TFR have positive relations. Moreover, as the number of waiting children rises, the TFR declines according to these regression results.

Case (8) includes the net migration rate as an independent variable; its estimated coefficient is 2.672, and it is statistically significant. It is difficult to interpret this result because municipalities with positive net migration rates are in urban areas, where the TFR might be lower than in rural areas. On the contrary, it could be interpreted that as young families increasingly move to urban areas, the TFR rises in those regions. Hence, who has migrated to another municipality is a key point to understand this result.

Case (12) is the most comprehensive result, showing that all the estimated coefficients of the independent variables except the female labor force participation rate are statistically significant. We obtain positive coefficients for child welfare expenses, the population of women aged 18–39 years, and the net migration rate and negative coefficients for population density, the number of waiting children, the percentage of unmarried women, and taxable income. It is difficult to understand why the estimated coefficient of the female labor force participation rate is not significant. From the coefficient of taxable income, it might be that demand for children declines as income increases following the hypothesis of population economics by Becker (1960) and Mincer (1963).

2.6.3 *Other Regression Results*

In this subsection, we show another regression result using a dataset from 2010. Although some municipalities merged between 2010 and 2015, we prepare the dataset based on 2010 for the same municipalities by adjusting such mergers. Hence, the two datasets (i.e., the 2010 dataset and 2015 dataset) represent the same municipality. The number of samples in both datasets is 1730. Treating the variables from the 2010 data as lagged variables and describing them using -1, we conduct our regression analysis using these lagged variables. Since there is a suspicion of endogeneity bias in the regressors, we lag the variables to avoid endogeneity.

Table 2.4 shows the regression results. The independent variables in Case (1) are population density and female labor force participation, which are both lagged variables. The estimated coefficient of population density is -0.007 (not statistically significant); hence, the lagged variable of population density does not influence the TFR. On the contrary, the estimated coefficient of female labor force participation is

Table 2.4 Estimation results for municipalities using lagged independent variables

	(1)	(2)	(3)	(4)	(5)	(6)	(7)	(8)
Const	1.329***	1.355***	1.406***	1.381***	1.365***	1.159***	1.185***	4.317***
	(0.109)	(0.099)	(0.099)	(0.101)	(0.108)	(0.081)	(0.079)	(0.441)
Population density (logarithm) (−1)	−0.007	−0.008	−0.028***	−0.024***	−0.025***	–	–	−0.010
	(0.006)	(0.006)	(0.007)	(0.007)	(0.008)	–	–	(0.007)
Female labor participation rate (−1)	0.317***	0.231**	0.260***	0.268***	0.331***	0.439***	0.365***	0.176**
	(0.100)	(0.097)	(0.098)	(0.099)	(0.097)	(0.095)	(0.102)	(0.083)
Capacity of nursery school (−1)	–	0.098**	0.080***	0.070**	–	–	0.076**	−0.001
	–	(0.028)	(0.028)	(0.029)	–	–	(0.030)	(0.028)
Ratio of child welfare expense to general tax revenue (−1)	–	–	0.348***	0.380***	0.411***	0.226***	0.201**	0.429***
	–	–	(0.106)	(0.103)	(0.104)	(0.082)	(0.082)	(0.105)
Number of waiting children to nursery school (−1)	–	–	–	−0.0003***	−0.0003***	−0.0003***	−0.0003***	−0.0002**
	–	–	–	(0.0001)	(0.0001)	(0.0001)	(0.0001)	(0.0001)
Taxable income (−1)	–	–	–	–	–	–	–	−0.371***
	–	–	–	–	–	–	–	(0.053)
Adjusted R^2	0.037	0.044	0.055	0.062	0.059	0.051	0.055	0.099
F value	33.81	27.39	26.24	23.98	28.09	32.06	26.26	32.69
Number of sample	1730	1730	1730	1730	1730	1730	1730	1730

Note Explained variable is TFR. White-Huber robust standard error in parentheses
In the table, *** means 1% significant, **means 5% significant, and * means 10% significant

0.317 and statistically significant. Case (3) includes five regressors, and all the estimated coefficients are statistically significant. The coefficient of population density is −0.024, and that of female labor force participation is 0.268. In addition, the estimated coefficients of nursery school capacity and child welfare expenses are 0.070 and 0.380, respectively.

Case (8) includes six independent variables, and the estimated coefficients of four of them are statistically significant. The estimated coefficient of female labor force participation is 0.176, that of child welfare expenses is 0.429, and that of the number of waiting children is −0.0002. In addition, taxable income has a negative coefficient (−0.371, statistically significant). Overall, although there are no large differences from the results in Table 2.3, the estimated coefficient of population density is not significant in some cases.

Table 2.5 shows another regression result using differenced variables (i.e., the regressor and regressands are the change from the value of the 2015 data to value of the 2010 data). Cases (1) to (3) show the basic results of these differenced regressions. The estimated coefficient of population density is positive, and that of the female labor force participation rate is negative in all cases in contrast to the results in Table 2.3 and Table 2.4. Hence, it is difficult to interpret these results.

Table 2.5 Estimation results for municipalities using differenced dependent variable

	(1)	(2)	(3)
Const	0.046***	0.043***	0.043***
	(0.005)	(0.005)	(0.005)
Population density (logarithm) (−1)	0.060***	0.039**	0.040**
	(0.017)	(0.017)	(0.017)
Female labor participation rate (−1)	−0.164**	−0.138**	−0.139**
	(0.070)	(0.066)	(0.067)
Capacity of nursery school (−1)	–	−0.048***	−0.048***
	–	(0.018)	(0.018)
Ratio of child welfare expense to general tax revenue (−1)	–	0.206***	0.206***
	–	(0.058)	(0.058)
Taxable income (−1)	–	–	-0.002
	–	–	(0.058)
Adjusted R^2	0.020	0.031	0.030
F value	18.30	14.67	11.73
Number of sample	1730	1730	1730

Note Explained variable is TFR which is differenced. White-Huber robust standard error in parentheses
In the table, *** means 1% significant, **means 5% significant, and * means 10% significant

2.7 Empirical Analysis 2: Multi-period Analysis

2.7.1 Pooled Data Analysis

We use two datasets for this multi-period analysis. One includes the TFR and other socioeconomic variables in 2015 and 2010 (corresponding to the data used in the previous analysis), and there are 1730 samples. The other is a three-period dataset that includes the TFR and other socioeconomic variables in 2005, 2010, and 2015. However, because there were many municipal mergers in the 2000s, we select municipalities that did not merge with other municipalities. As a result, the number of samples in the three-period dataset is 1464.

In this subsection, the two-period dataset that consists of 1730 samples in 2010 and 2015 is used for the pooled analysis. Table 2.6 shows the pooled regression results. Case (1) is the basic result, which confirms that the estimated coefficient of population density is negative and that of female labor force participation is positive, similar to the result in the previous section. Case (3) corresponds to Case (1) in Table 2.3. Here, the estimated coefficients are much closer to each other. Although the coefficient of nursery school capacity is not statistically significant in Case (1) of Table 2.3, it is now statistically significant. In the next subsection, we discuss this different result.

In Case (4), all the independent variables are consistent from a theoretical point of view and statistically significant. The estimated coefficient of nursery school capacity is positive and statistically significant. Lastly, Case (8) includes taxable income as in Case (4) and the coefficient is negative, consistent with the previous analysis. In conclusion, the estimation results using pooled data are almost the same as the results using only 2015 data.

2.7.2 Three-Period Analysis

Table 2.7 shows the regression results of each period as well as the pooled regression result. The column headed "2015 full DB" shows the results obtained using the 1730 samples as in Table 2.3. The left side of Table 2.7 indicates the estimation results for four independent variables, and the right side shows the results with taxable income included as well.

On the left side of Table 2.7, the regression results are almost the same; however, the estimated coefficients of the independent variables do differ slightly. Firstly, the results of "2015 full DB" and "2015" are close and not statistically significant for nursery school capacity. However, using the data in 2010 and 2005, the estimated coefficient of nursery school capacity is statistically significant in contrast to the data in 2015. Hence, providing nursery school availability is effective at raising the TFR in 2010 and 2005. On the contrary, the same policy is not effective in 2015. These

Table 2.6 Estimation results of pooling data in 2010 and in 2015

	(1)	(2)	(3)	(4)	(5)	(6)	(7)	(8)
Const	1.362***	1.385***	1.431***	1.405***	1.395***	1.083***	1.100***	4.282***
	(0.066)	(0.063)	(0.064)	(0.065)	(0.065)	(0.051)	(0.052)	(0.322)
Population density (logarithm)	−0.013***	−0.014***	−0.040***	−0.036***	−0.037***	–	–	−0.024***
	(0.004)	(0.004)	(0.005)	(0.005)	(0.005)	–	–	(0.005)
Female labor participation rate	0.281***	0.215***	0.279***	0.288***	0.323***	0.486***	0.442***	0.189***
	(0.057)	(0.059)	(0.062)	(0.062)	(0.058)	(0.058)	(0.066)	(0.055)
Capacity of nursery school	–	0.072**	0.048**	0.036*	–	–	0.043**	−0.029
	–	(0.019)	(0.020)	(0.020)	–	–	(0.021)	(0.020)
Ratio of child welfare expense to general tax revenue	–	–	0.458***	0.513***	0.529***	0.284***	0.269***	0.561***
	–	–	(0.077)	(0.076)	(0.075)	(0.059)	(0.060)	(0.077)
Number of waiting children to nursery school	–	–	–	−0.0004***	−0.0004***	−0.0004***	−0.0004***	−0.0003***
	–	–	–	(0.0001)	(0.0001)	(0.0001)	(0.0001)	(0.0001)
Taxable income	–	–	–	–	–	–	–	−0.362***
	–	–	–	–	–	–	–	(0.039)
Dummy for 2015	0.013	0.001	0.002	0.001	0.001	-0.005	-0.005	0.016**
	(0.008)	(0.008)	(0.008)	(0.008)	(0.008)	(0.008)	(0.008)	(0.008)
Adjusted R^2	0.052	0.056	0.062	0.090	0.089	0.071	0.073	0.127
F value	64.36	52.49	29.47	57.92	68.65	67.37	55.11	72.85
Number of sample	3460	3460	3460	3460	3460	3460	3460	3460

Note Explained variable is TFR. White-Huber robust standard error in parentheses
In the table, *** means 1% significant, **means 5% significant, and * means 10% significant

Table 2.7 Comparison of estimation results using 2005, 2010, and 2015 data

	2015 full DB	2015	2010	2005	Pool	2015 full DB	2015	2010	2005	Pool
Const	1.388***	1.397***	1.462***	1.404***	1.411***	4.180***	4.073***	4.758***	5.088***	4.469***
	(0.085)	(0.091)	(0.103)	(0.093)	(0.053)	(0.459)	(0.494)	(0.448)	(0.398)	(0.249)
Population density (logarithm)	−0.035***	−0.033***	−0.040***	−0.047***	−0.044***	−0.024***	−0.022***	−0.023***	−0.023***	−0.025***
	(0.007)	(0.007)	(0.008)	(0.007)	(0.004)	(0.007)	(0.007)	(0.007)	(0.007)	(0.004)
Female labor participation rate	0.302***	0.282***	0.251**	0.342***	0.320***	0.197***	0.184**	0.157*	0.228***	0.205***
	(0.077)	(0.080)	(0.100)	(0.088)	(0.047)	(0.074)	(0.078)	(0.082)	(0.073)	(0.042)
Capacity of nursery school	0.024	0.030	0.084***	0.068**	0.054***	−0.038	−0.003	−0.003	−0.018	−0.016
	(0.027)	(0.029)	(0.032)	(0.033)	(0.018)	(0.028)	(0.030)	(0.030)	(0.033)	(0.017)
Ratio of child welfare expense to general tax revenue	0.516***	0.450***	0.319***	0.410***	0.499***	0.579***	0.514***	0.388***	0.373***	0.472***
	(0.107)	(0.108)	(0.111)	(0.144)	(0.060)	(0.109)	(0.111)	(0.113)	(0.134)	(0.056)
Taxable income	–	–	–	–	–	−0.349***	−0.334***	−0.418***	−0.464***	−0.385***
	–	–	–	–	–	(0.056)	(0.060)	(0.055)	(0.048)	(0.030)
Adjusted R^2	0.062	0.059	0.092	0.176	0.129	0.099	0.094	0.140	0.239	0.177
F value	29.47	24.01	38.22	79.17	163.59	39.00	31.42	48.56	93.11	189.28
Number of sample	1730	1464	1464	1464	4392	1730	1464	1464	1464	4392

Note Explained variable is TFR. White-Huber robust standard error in parentheses
In the table, *** means 1% significant, **means 5% significant, and * means 10% significant

results suggest that the policy to increase nursery school capacity itself has been insufficient to raise the TFR in 2015; in other words, its purpose has been achieved.

In the case of "pool" on the left side, which means the three-period pooled analysis, the number of samples is 4392. The estimated coefficient of population density is −0.044, and that of female labor force participation is 0.320 (both statistically significant). In addition, the estimated coefficient of child welfare expenses is 0.499 and is statistically significant. The results on the right side of Table 2.7 are generally consistent with those on the left side. In the pooled data, the estimated coefficient of taxable income is -0.385 and that of population density is −0.025, which is little weaker than the case without taxable income. Further, the estimated coefficient of female labor force participation is slightly lower than the case without taxable income. Lastly, Table 2.8 shows the results when we add a period dummy variable, estimated using fixed-effect regression. Cases (1) and (2) correspond to those in Table 2.7, and the estimation results are similar in both.

Table 2.8 Estimation results of panel regression

	(1)	(2)	(3)	(4)
Const	1.440***	4.640***	1.431***	4.639***
	(0.059)	(0.268)	(0.043)	(0.207)
Population density (logarithm)	−0.043***	−0.026***	−0.043***	−0.026***
	(0.004)	(0.004)	(0.004)	(0.004)
Female labor participation rate	0.288***	0.185***	0.289***	0.186***
	(0.052)	(0.045)	(0.039)	(0.038)
Capacity of nursery school	0.057***	−0.021	0.057***	−0.021
	(0.018)	(0.018)	(0.016)	(0.017)
Ratio of child welfare expense to general tax revenue	0.437***	0.485***	0.438***	0.486***
	(0.067)	(0.067)	(0.044)	(0.043)
Taxable income	–	−0.403***	–	−0.404***
	–	(0.033)	–	(0.025)
Dummy for 2005 data	−0.025***	−0.001	–	–
	(0.010)	(0.009)	–	–
Dummy for 2010 data	−0.002	−0.018**	–	–
	(0.008)	(0.008)	–	–
Method	Pooled	Pooled	Fixed	Fixed
Adjusted R^2	0.131	0.178	0.132	0.179
F value	111.19	136.47	111.12	136.52
Number of sample	4392	4392	4392	4392

Note: Explained variable is TFR. White-Huber robust standard error in parentheses
In the table, *** means 1% significant, **means 5% significant, and * means 10% significant

2.8 Concluding Remarks

This study considered the background of the disparity in the TFR in Japan by municipality. The disparity in the TFR between municipalities is large, with the highest TFR 2.47 and the lowest TFR 0.84 at the municipality level in 2015 (data from 2013 to 2017). The large disparity in the TFR at the municipality level is driven by the differences in children-related costs, the work/life balance between employment and child-rearing for young families, the existence of a young population, and the policies of municipalities.

It is often reported that the TFR is relatively low in municipalities with high population density. Hence, we considered population density as a proxy variable for children-related costs and conducted an empirical analysis focusing on the relationship between population density and the TFR. Furthermore, the female labor force participation rate was used as a proxy variable for an environment in which employment and child-rearing are compatible and flexible for female workers and young families. In addition, we adopted the ratio of young women to the total population to represent the age structure in the municipality as well as variables such as child welfare expenses, nursery school capacity, and the number of waiting children to account for the fertility rate improvement policy by municipalities.

In this study, based on TFR data by municipality in 2015 (2013–2017) published by the Ministry of Health, Labour and Welfare, we examine the relationship between the TFR and socioeconomic variables obtained from the Population Census in 2015. The number of samples is 1730. In addition to the above dataset, pooled data including the TFR and socioeconomic variables in 2010 (2008–2012) and a three-period dataset including data on 2015, 2010, and 2005 (2003–2007) are used in the empirical analysis.

The empirical analyses show that the estimated coefficient of population density is negative, while that of female labor force participation is positive; both are statistically significant. These findings suggest that children-related costs have a negative influence, while a compatible environment has a positive influence on the TFR. It is also shown that the existence of many young families and the government's policy for raising the TFR have a positive effect, whereas the increase in the number of waiting children has a negative effect on the TFR. This study is a cross-sectional analysis and does not find causal relationships; it merely indicates the existence of a correlation.

This study aimed to clarify the background of the TFR disparity by municipality. The empirical analyses confirmed that the TFR disparity is driven by children-related costs, the structure of the population, and the policies of municipalities. In the future, we would like to analyze this topic to find the precise causal relationships.

References

Abe, K., & Harada, Y. (2008). Kosodate-Siensaku no Syusshou Ritu ni Ataeru Eikilyou. *Kaikei Kensa Kenkilyu,38*, 1–16. (in Japanese).

Alvarez Diaz, M., D'hombres, B., Ghisetti, C., Pontarollo, N., & Dijkstra, L. (2018). The determinants of population growth—literature review and empirical analysis. JRC Working Papers in Economics and Finance, 2018/10, Publications Office of the European Union.

Adachi, Y., & Nakazato, T. (2017). Syusshou Ritu no Kettei Youin—Todoufuken betu data niyoru Bunseki. *Nihon Keizai Kenkilyu, 75*, 63–91 (in Japanese).

Becker, G. S. (1960). An economic analysis of fertility. In A. Coale (Ed.), *Universities-National Bureau Conference Series No.11*. Princeton University Press.

Croix, D., & Gobbi, P. (2015). *Population density, fertility, and demographic convergence in developing countries, IRES discussion papers, No.3*. Université Catholique de Louvain.

Croix, D., & Gobbi, P. (2017). Population density, fertility, and demographic convergence in developing countries. *Journal of Development Economics, 127*, 13–24.

Kamata, K., & Iwasawa, M. (2009). Spatial variations in fertility: Geographically weighted regression analyses for town-and-village-level TFR in Japan. *Population Studies, 45*, 1–20. (in Japanese).

Kato, H. (2018). The analysis on disparities of fertility rate of Japanese municipalities. *Public Policy Review, Policy Research Institute, Ministry of Finance, 14*(1), 1–24.

Lutz, W., & Qiang, R. (2002). Determinants of human population growth. *Philosophical Transactions of the Royal Society B: Biological Science, 357*, 1197–1210.

Lutz, W., Testa, M., & Penn, D. (2006). Population density is a key factor in declining human fertility. *Population Environment, 28*(2), 69–81.

Mincer, J. (1963). Market prices, opportunity costs, and income effects. In C. Christ, et al. (Eds.), *Measurement in economics: Studies in mathematical economics and econometrics in memory of Yehuda Grunfeld*. University Press.

Nishimoto, M., & Suruga, T. (2011). Chiiki Data ni yoru Bankonka, Shousika no Bunseki, the Hannan ronshu. *Social Science, Hannan University, 46*(2), 19–39. (in Japanese).

Sato, Y. (2007). Economic geography, fertility and migration. *Journal of Urban Economics, 61*, 372–387.

Tanabe, K., & Suzuki, T. (2016). Todofuken no Syusshou Ritu Kakusa no Bunseki. *Kousei no Sihiyo,63*(5), 13–21. (in Japanese).

Tang, S., & Chen, L. (2002). Density-dependent birth rate, birth pulses and their population dynamic consequences. *Journal of Mathematical Biology, 44*, 185–199.

Unayama, S., & Yamamoto G. (2015). *Hoikusho no Seibi to Jiyosei no Rodouryoku Ritu, Syusshou Ritu, PRI discussion paper series, No.15A-2*. Policy Research Institute, Ministry Of Finance. (in Japanese).

Chapter 3
Total Fertility Rate, Economic–Social Conditions, and Public Policies in OECD Countries

Abstract A long-term decline trend in the TFR has been observed in almost all the OECD countries, although there are differences in the country-level or speed of change. Many factors cause the decline in the TFR. However, there are common factors in OECD countries, despite many different social and economic backgrounds. Thus, this chapter explores these common factors using panel econometrics analysis. Furthermore, this research is distinguished from the past studies by other researchers as it confirms the effectiveness of government policy tools in improving TFR. This research uses balanced panel data for OECD countries from 1986 to 2017 and prepares several different balanced panel datasets. To explore all factors that determine birth behavior is almost impossible because several variables are related to the TFR. Therefore, we chose four kinds of variables: labor market, macroeconomic environments, political tools, and demographic conditions. The empirical results using the basic dataset are not statistically significant in a fixed-effect model with more explanatory variables. However, while the female labor participation (FLP) rate correlates positively with TFR in the simple pooling model, the female unemployment rate (FUR) negatively impacts TFR, being statistically significant in all cases. As for the macroeconomic environment, the GDP per capita affects TFR negatively, and on the other side the economic growth rate positively affects the TFR. It can be interpreted that the expectation for better economic circumstances in the future improves the decision to have children. Furthermore, while the coefficient of the length of maternity and parental leave has negative signs, social expenditure has a positive influence on the TFR. Lastly, the estimated coefficient of the demographic variable, that is, the young female population ratio to the total population and the ratio of a child born out of wedlock, is positive. Additionally, we estimated the dynamic panel model. However, the lagged variable of TFR explains the current TFR. Additionally, we estimate using the AR model. It is required to show the time series characteristics to deal with such series. More concretely, stationarity is a necessary condition to estimate the time series model. Confirming the unit root test for main variables, we concluded that those variables contain a unit root, and there is no cointegration among them. We confirmed the same conclusions using different variables, as in the level variables.

H. Kato, *Macro-econometric Analysis on Determinants of Fertility Behavior*, Population Studies of Japan, https://doi.org/10.1007/978-981-16-3927-2_3

Keywords Total fertility rate · Social expenditures · Labor participation · Panel analysis · Panel unit root · Panel cointegration

3.1 Introduction

The long-term trend of declining total fertility rate (TFR) has been observed in almost all OECD countries, although there are differences in country-level or speed of change. As of 2020, OECD consisted of 37 countries; the simple average value of the TFR in those countries was 1.63 in 2018, much lower than the level that can maintain the current population. For reference, the level of TFR three decades ago was 1.95 in 1990. As mentioned above, there are large disparities among OECD countries. The highest TFR of OECD countries was 3.09 in Israel, 2.13 in Mexico, and 1.99 in Turkey. In contrast, the lowest TFR was 0.98 in Korea, 1.26 in Spain, and 1.29 in Italy. Figure 3.1 shows the level of TFR in the OECD countries in 2018.

Many factors are considered as the cause of the declining TFR. However, there should be common factors in OECD countries, despite many differences in social and economic backgrounds. This research explores these common factors using panel econometrics analysis. Many previous studies attempted to identify the common factors of declining TFR in developed countries. This research is distinguished from the past studies by other researchers as follows. First, our study finds social and economic factors which affect birth behavior, and confirms the effectiveness of government policy tools to improve the TFR. Second, after scrutinizing our panel data characteristics, we estimate reliable relations between the TFR and government policies using appropriate procedures.

The common factors affecting the declining TFR include the female labor market, macroeconomic environment, demographic conditions, and political interventions, which are important variables in developed countries. From the long-term history of researching birth behavior by economics, the opportunity cost of children is an important factor in understanding the TFR changes. Without an appropriate environment, such as a compatible support system between childcare and the job for young families, female wage progress according to economic maturity becomes a serious opportunity cost. This is related to labor participation by the female population. Additionally, the long-term sustainable economic growth may affect the improvement of the TFR. However, continuous recession worsens conditions for young couples to have children. Furthermore, a demographic situation such as a shrinking young population may affect birth behavior via marriages. Additionally, political tools affect the TFR by improving the childcare environment.

This chapter emphasizes the analysis and measures the effectiveness of government intervention in childbirth behavior. Public expenditure and other benefits such as parental leave are the main interests to analyze economically and objectively. Public spending by the government is classified into two categories, cash benefits such as

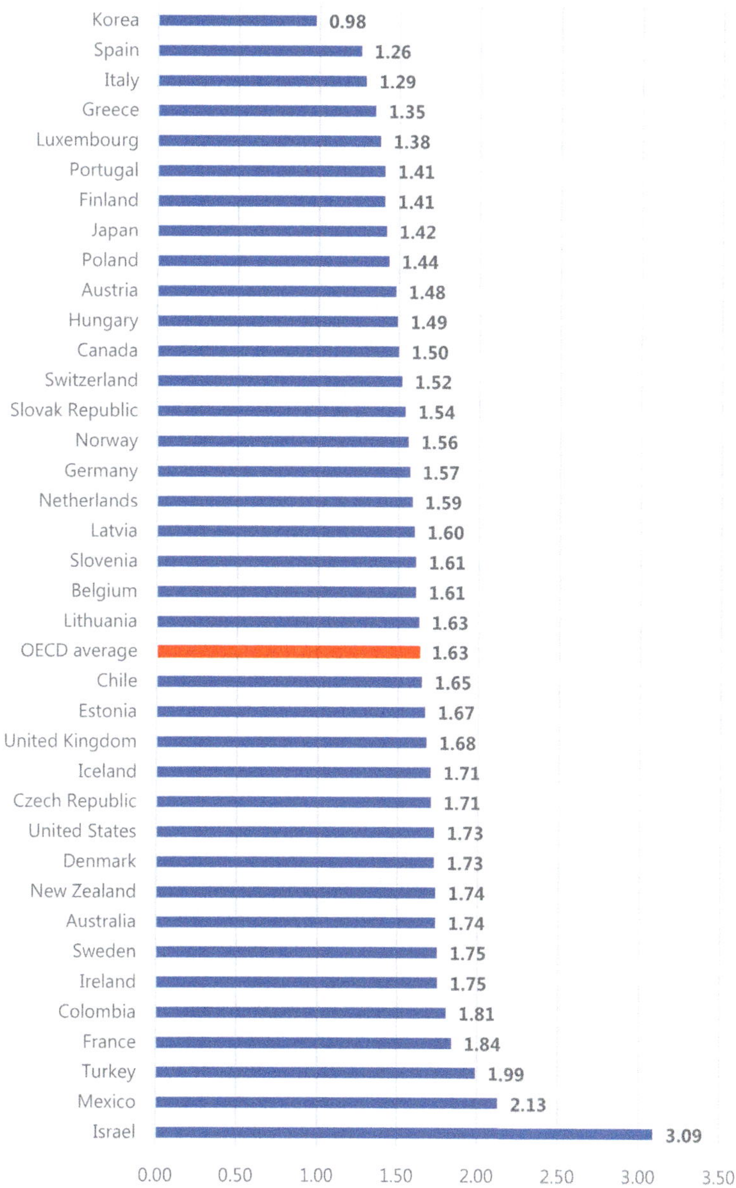

Fig. 3.1 TFR in 2018. *Source* OECD database

children's allowances and in-kind benefits such as improving the childcare environment. Furthermore, although it is difficult to grasp measurable variables, gender equality is an important factor that affects TFR changes in the OECD countries.

This research uses balanced panel data of the OECD countries from 1986 to 2017. A balanced dataset includes necessary data of all countries at all times. Long-term data for the OECD countries are available, and more historical data would make it an unbalanced dataset. Unbalanced data are one where certain years or certain countries are not observed. The unbalanced panel dataset where some data are lost randomly has the same information as the balanced data; however, the missing data in the OECD dataset are related to the year of joining by a country; thus, those are not random. Therefore, we should build balanced datasets. Additionally, balanced panel data are appropriate to analyze the time series characteristics. We prepared several balanced panel datasets in this research, explained in the following section.

This chapter is organized as follows. The next section summarizes the prior literature related to our theme. Section 3.3 shows the primary data, such as the TFR and other socioeconomic variables, mainly labor market, macroeconomic, and policy-related variables, and Sect. 3.4 provides estimation results of the impact of socioeconomic conditions and effectiveness of policy variables. Particularly, we are interested in how public spending expenditure on young families affects the TFR. Section 3.5 discusses the time series characteristics of our panel data and attempts to estimate difference series data. We obtain the same conclusions regarding the impact of political variables on TFR as in the previous section. Concluding remarks are given in Sect. 3.6.

3.2 Literature

Many previous researches show that this theme has attracted the interest of economists and demographers. We introduce representative papers from the perspective of panel estimation results and policy implications.

D'Addio and D'Ercole (2005) is a representative paper on this theme. They collected data consisting of 16 OECD countries from 1980 to 1999 and showed that higher public transfers to families reduce the costs for children and raise the TFR. Although they found that a longer parental leave lowers fertility rates, they could not interpret it easily as parental leave was an important tool to help young families. Additionally, the estimated coefficient of female unemployment rate on TFR was negative, and that of the employment rate on TFR was positive.

Gauthier and Hatzius (1997) adopted dynamic panel analysis for 22 OECD countries covering the period 1970–1990 and showed that direct cash benefit had positive and significant effects on the TFR. However, the female unemployment rate had no significant effect, in contrast to D'Addio and D'Ercole (2005). Adserá (2004) used unbalanced panel data of 23 countries from 1960 to 1997 and found that the unemployment rate and income level (GDP) negatively impact the TFR. The length of maternity leave had no significant impact.

Thévenon (2011) and Luci-Greulich and Thévenon (2013) are also representative papers in this theme. Luci-Greulich and Thévenon (2013) gathered data from 18 OECD countries for the period 1982–2007. They found that family policy had a positive impact on the TFR. For example, there is a positive impact of income support over childhood on fertility and a positive relationship between the length of maternity leave and the TFR. The relation between TFR and GDP per capita was estimated to be a U-shaped relation. This means that an increase of GDP per capita decreases the TFR for initial economic development. Still, after the economy has matured, an increased GDP per capita is accompanied by an increase in TFR. Lechman, Dominiak, and Okonowicz (2014) also found a similar relation between TFR and economic growth. They proposed a U-shaped trajectory in the long-run TFR trends determined by economic growth using data from 18 developed countries between 1970 and 2011. Olivetti and Petrongolo (2017) showed that public spending on family benefits and the duration of paid child-related leave for mothers was significantly associated with an increase in TFR, using data from 22 OECD countries in 1970–2010. Besides, Rovny (2011) found that maternity and parental leave for the Nordic countries and France were positive for TFR.

Family policies have a positive impact on TFR. However, Castles (2003) stated that social expenditure does not impact fertility rates. Hondroyiannis (2010) analyzed panel data from nonstationarity and tested unbalanced panel data for 27 EU countries for the period 1990–2005 using the panel unit root test and showed that the variables in his research had unit roots. The results showed that the income and opportunity cost of children did not affect the TFR.

3.3 TFR and Related Data

This section shows the trend and the data of factors that seem to affect TFR in OECD countries.

3.3.1 Changes of TFR in OECD Countries

Figure 3.1 shows the current TFR level in the OECD countries. Additionally, to grasp the trends of the TFR change, Fig. 3.2a and b shows a long-term transition of the selected 29 countries. We excluded eight countries that joined the OECD recently from the above two graphs. Furthermore, we divided the 29 countries into two groups considering the level of TFR in 2018.

Figure 3.2a shows that the TFR level for high TFR countries stayed between 1.5 and 2.5 from 1990 to 2018, except for some countries. Although the TFR level increased slightly from the mid-2000s, it has recently decreased and remained at the same level as in the 1990s. The characteristic point is that the TFR of Mexico and Turkey is declining rapidly, and the TFR of the Czech Republic is recovering rapidly.

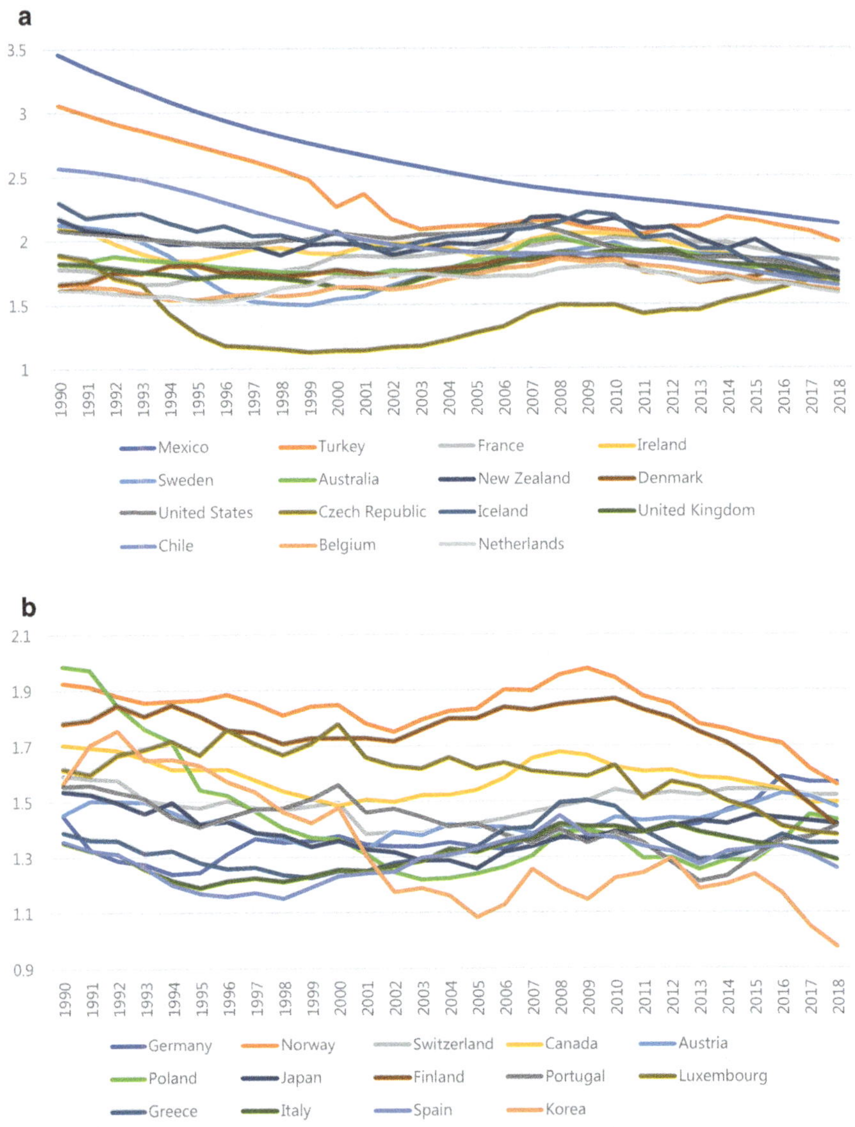

Fig. 3.2 **a** TFR changes in high TFR countries. **b** TFR changes in low TFR countries. *Source* OECD database

For countries with relatively low fertility rates, as in Fig. 3.2b, their TFR remained in the range of less than 2.0 and did not show a large decline except in Norway, Finland, and South Korea. Norway and Finland have seen rapid declines in the TFR since the mid-2000s. South Korea is the only country in the OECD with a TFR of less than 1.0 in 2018. For references, the simple average of TFR in the 29 OECD countries was

1.88 in 1990 and 1.68 in 2000. After that, the average TFR had improved slightly to 1.75 in 2010; however, it started to decline again and fell to 1.58 in 2018.

3.3.2 Considering Factors with TFR

It is almost impossible to explore all factors that determine birth behavior by young families because there are many variables related to TFR. Furthermore, it may not be useful to describe the relationship between the multitudes of variables and TFR by trial and error. Therefore, we chose four kinds of variables: labor market, macroeconomic environments, political tools, and demographic conditions.

The FLP or employment rate, unemployment rate, work style, part-time job, and wage difference between males and females are crucial factors for labor market-related variables. The correlation between the TFR and the FLP has been controversial, for example, D'Addio and Mira d'Ercole (2005). We focus on the impacts of these variables on the TFR in the following sections, showing estimation results. Economic environments are indispensable variables that influence the decision-making of birth. Optimistic expectations for the future contribute to family formation and vice versa. Therefore, the current economic situation becomes one of the factors influencing the decision to have children. Therefore, this study adopted variables such as the GDP growth rate and the level of per capita GDP.

Additionally, political tools are important factors that affect TFR changes, and this variable plays a crucial role in this research. As mentioned in the Introduction, we contribute to this field by examining the effectiveness of government policy. The representative index of political contribution in improving the TFR is the degree of public spending on young families, including cash benefit, which helps the financial predicament of raising children, and in-kind benefit, which supports child-raising. Parental leave should also be considered in the analysis. Additionally, demographic conditions are necessary variables, the female share among the young population which might affect marriage. The following subsections introduce the data in OECD countries.

3.3.3 Female Labor Market and TFR

The discussion of the relation between the FLP and the TFR is ongoing. It is understood that this relationship may depend on appropriate female working environments for balancing work with raising children. For example, D'Addio and Mira d'Ercole (2005) showed that the relationship changed in the mid-1990s, from a negative to positive relation. Correlations in a specific year between the FLP of those aged 20–54 years and the TFR are calculated for the 29 OECD countries, excluding Mexico and Turkey, because the TFR of both countries showed unusual transition than other countries. In 1996, the correlation of it was 0.087 and not statistically significant;

the relation between the two variables was not observed. In 2005, the correlation became 0.263, and that was positive, but not significant. In 2018, it was 0.360 and statistically significant. Although these are not the same result as in D'Addio and Mira d'Ercole (2005), the conclusion that the relationship between the two variables became gradually positive is confirmed.

Although female unemployment is an important factor affecting the TFR, how it affects TFR cannot be determined in advance.

Deterioration of working opportunities makes economic conditions worse and negatively influences the decision to have children. However, the increasing unemployment rate works to lengthen childcare hours at home, reduces the opportunity cost of children, and increases TFR. Therefore, we cannot assume the sign of the variable, unemployment rate of female, in the empirical analysis. Additionally, working conditions such as nonregular jobs have the same influence as unemployment because an increasing share of female part-time jobs means deterioration of their working opportunities. We consider the aforementioned discussions in our analysis. The variables introduced here were obtained from the OECD database.

3.3.4 Macroeconomic Conditions and TFR

From the perspective of population economics, children seem like economic goods; hence, income condition is an indispensable factor in determining the demand for children. Specifically, we chose economic growth rate and income level per capita as macroeconomic variables in the analysis. The economic growth rate was measured as the increase of nominal GDP by national currency obtained from the OECD database. The GDP per capita was obtained from "Penn World Table, version 10.0." We calculated it as the expenditure-side real GDP at chained purchasing power parity (PPP) (in mil. 2017 US$) and divided it by the total population for each country. Figure 3.3 shows the negative relation between the GDP per capita and the economic growth rate on average from 1995 to 2017 in 27 OECD countries. A country with high GDP per capita measured a relatively lower economic growth rate, and the correlation coefficient was −0.395.

From the observations of past empirical analysis, as the macroeconomy matures, the demand for children declines, and the TFR decreases. However, a high economic growth rate contributes to the households' economic condition better; thus, it is expected that the economic growth rate and TFR have positive relations. Furthermore, the current economic growth rate becomes a proxy indicator in predicting future economic conditions by young families. If the young families have optimistic visions for the future, they could decide to have children.

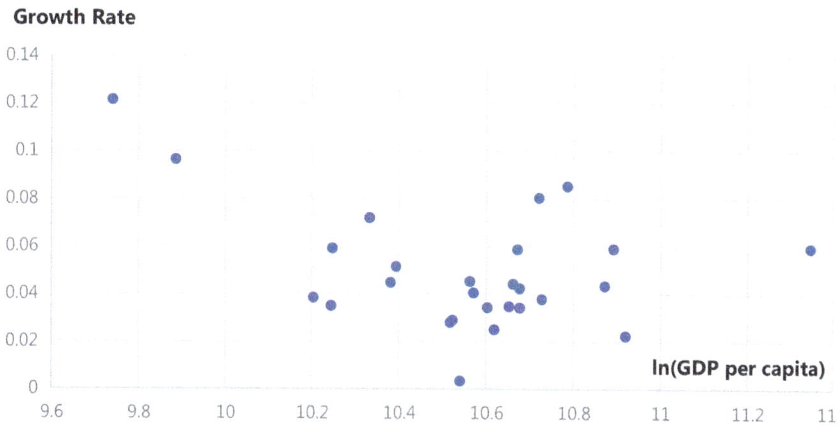

Fig. 3.3 Economic growth rate versus GDP per capita. *Source* OECD database and "Penn World Table, version 10.0." *Note* Average from 1995 to 2017 in 27 OECD countries. Country list: Australia, Austria, Belgium, Canada, Chile, Czech Republic, Denmark, Finland, France, Germany, Greece, Iceland, Ireland, Italy, Japan, Korea, Luxembourg, Netherlands, New Zealand, Norway, Poland, Portugal, Spain, Sweden, Switzerland, UK, and USA

3.3.5 The Government Policies and TFR

Improving TFR in the OECD countries is a difficult and urgent task for governments. Hence, they have implemented several kinds of policies to improve the TFR. For example, public spending on young families or maternity and parental leaves are the main features in almost all countries. Here, we use social expenditure on families from the OECD dataset of "Social Expenditure—Aggregated data." These data include public spending by cash benefit and in-kind benefit, both measured as a GDP ratio and used as proxy variables for government support to improve the TFR.

To confirm the effectiveness of social expenditure on TFR, we estimate the simple correlation coefficient among the 30 OECD countries. Notably, although 29 OECD countries were targeted in the above section, we added Israel, as data were available; hence, the number of targeted countries is 30. Figure 3.4 shows the relationships between the TFR and social expenditure for a family, the total public expenditure, including cash and in-kind benefits. In the case of 30 countries, the correlation coefficient was only 0.15. However, in 27 countries, excluding Mexico, Turkey, and Israel, the correlation coefficient was 0.59.

We estimated using a simple panel regression to explore more detailed impacts of social expenditure on the TFR among these 30 countries. The result that there exists a significant positive relationship is shown in Table 3.1. However, we obtained different results while classifying the expenditure as cash benefit and in-kind benefit. Before explaining the results, we introduce the data and method. We chose the simple pooling regression and fixed-effect estimation using the data obtained from the 30 countries during 1995–2017.

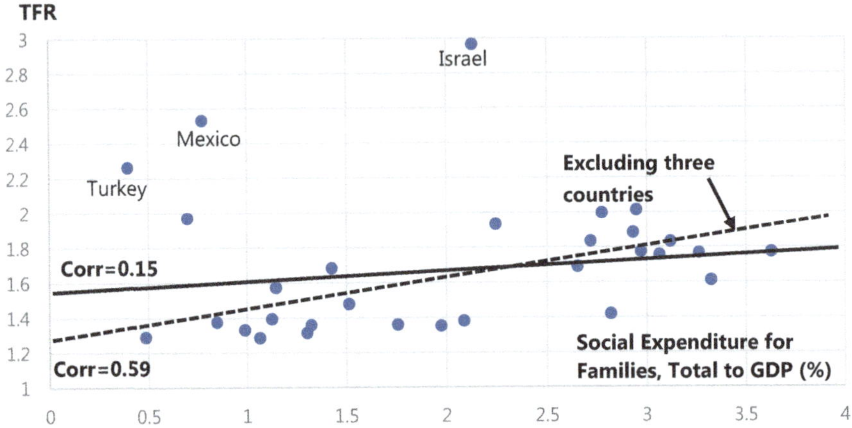

Fig. 3.4 TFR and social expenditure for families. *Source* OECD data https://data.oecd.org/. *Note* Values are an average from 1995 to 2017

Table 3.1 Social expenditure and TFR

Dependent var: TFR

	Case (1)	Case (2)	Case (3)	Case (4)	Case (5)	Case (6)
Const	1.5823***	1.6146***	1.6766***	1.6204***	1.5779***	1.6982***
	(0.0331)	(0.0278)	(0.0302)	(0.0222)	(0.0251)	(0.0160)
Total	0.0620***	0.0457***	–	–	–	–
	(0.0149)	(0.0139)	–	–	–	–
Cash	–	–	0.0234	0.0694***	–	–
	–	–	(0.0214)	(0.0179)	–	–
In-kind	–	–	–	–	0.1672***	0.0091
	–	–	–	–	(0.0267)	(0.0203)
Method	Pool	Fixed	Pool	Fixed	Pool	Fixed
F statistics	–	276.38	-	278.23	–	276.38
Adj. R^2	0.001	0.923	0.001	0.923	0.3990	0.3150

Note In the table, *** means 1% significant, **means 5% significant, and * means 10% significant
Standard error in parentheses. Period: 1995–2017, country: 30, total observation: 690
Country list: Australia, Austria, Belgium, Canada, Chile, Czech Republic, Denmark, Finland, France, Germany, Greece, Iceland, Ireland, Israel, Italy, Japan, Korea, Luxembourg, Mexico, Netherlands, New Zealand, Norway, Poland, Portugal, Spain, Sweden, Switzerland, Turkey, UK, and USA

Cases (1) and (2) show that total social expenditure for families has a positive and statistically significant effect on the TFR, and the estimated coefficient of Case (2) was 0.0457.

However, the effect of cash benefit is significant in Case (4) of fixed-effect estimation and not significant in Case (3) of pooling estimation. However, the in-kind benefit was significant in Case (5) of pooling estimation but not significant in Case (6) of fixed-effect estimation. In general, it is considered that in-kind benefit is more effective than cash benefit in the economic context because in-kind benefit has an impact directly on the choice to have children by young families, as in Kato (2011). From the results of Table 3.1, the fixed-effect estimation would be more reliable. Cash benefit has a positive and significant effect on improving the TFR. We confirm this in the next section.

3.4 Impact of Socioeconomic Conditions and Public Policies on TFR

In this chapter, using three different balanced panel datasets of the OECD countries, we measure the impact of socioeconomic conditions and public policies on TFR.

3.4.1 Introduction of the Three-Panel Dataset

As several factors influence the TFR, socioeconomic data are required for the empirical analysis. However, it is difficult to gather long-term and comprehensive data for all countries without missing values in the OECD database. There are many uncontrollable reasons such as missing data source or difference in the joining year of each country to OECD. Furthermore, as we have mentioned above, we should use balanced panel data to analyze cross-country data. We prepared three different kinds of panel datasets to satisfy these difficult conditions, and each dataset included different countries and different periods to other datasets.

Dataset A is the base dataset, which contains data of 30 OECD countries from 1995 to 2017, and basic variables of the labor market, macroeconomic environments, political tools, and demographic conditions are included. Dataset B is the longest period data among our three datasets. However, we could not obtain data of some countries in Dataset A. Dataset B includes 18 OECD countries from 1986 to 2017, and this dataset has a limited number of policy-related variables. Additionally, we created Dataset C, the shortest period dataset but the most data-rich. Although Dataset C contains data from only 14 countries and the sample period is from 2001 to 2016, it has many policy-related variables. We proceed with the following empirical analysis by using these three datasets appropriately. A list of countries included in each dataset is provided in the appendix.

3.4.2 Long-Term Balanced Panel

In this subsection, the estimation results using long-term balanced panel dataset, that is, Dataset A, are shown in Tables 3.2 and 3.3. Table 3.2 shows basic results using various estimation methods. As explained above, this dataset contains data of 30 OECD countries from 1995 to 2017; 690 samples are in common in Table 3.2.

In Cases (1)–(4), we adopted common independent variables such as the FLP, female unemployment rate (FUR), GDP per capita (GDPP), and social expenditure for families (including both cash benefit and in-kind benefit, SE). A different estimation method was used among these four cases: pooling model, fixed-effect model (with and without time dummy), and random effect model. Excluding FLP, we obtained signs of the estimated statistically significant coefficients, consistent with the above hypothesis in the four cases; that is, the sign of the estimated coefficient of FUP and GDPP was negative, and SE was positive. The deteriorating labor market for females and increasing economic maturity reduced TFR, and the government support for young families was effective in improving TFR. The Case (1) pooling model was the only case where the coefficient was statistically significant for FLP. Regarding estimation methods for Cases (2) and (4), the fixed-effect model was chosen for the Hausman test, not the random effect model. However, the test statistics were small, and there might be some reservations about the conclusion. Additionally, the time dummy of Case (3) did not affect the result compared to Case (2).

In Cases (5)–(7), the GDPG rate was chosen as an independent variable instead of GDP per capita, and the results were different from the above cases. The estimated coefficient of GDPG was positive and statistically significant, meaning that improving the current economic environment effectively improved the TFR. Therefore, for Cases (5) and (7), the random effect model was chosen for the Hausman test. However, in Case (7), the p-value was 0.102; thus, the selection of the estimation method may not be appropriate. Also, the time dummy variable in Case (6) did not affect the result compared to Case (5).

In Cases (8) and (9), although both GDPP and GDPG were included as dependent variables simultaneously, the coefficient of GDPP was negative but not significant. The random effect model was chosen for the Hausman test of Case (9); however, the p-value was not large. It is difficult to determine the appropriate estimation method. The selection of the fixed-effect model or random effect model becomes a subtle decision. Considering that data characteristics are national, country-based, it may be preferred that the fixed-effect model is chosen. We use the fixed-effect model as the standard estimation method hereafter.

Next, the effects of government policy in improving TFR are observed in more detail. Cases (1) and (5) in Table 3.3 are similar to Cases (2) and (5) in Table 3.2, respectively. The other cases in Table 3.3 show the effect of social expenditure, classified as cash benefit and in-kind benefit. Interestingly, cash benefit was effective, meaning the estimated coefficient of the variable is positive and statistically significant. However, the in-kind benefit was not. In Cases (2) and (4), the estimated values

Table 3.2 Estimation results: basic cases

Dependent var: TFR

	(1)	(2)	(3)	(4)	(5)	(6)	(7)	(8)	(9)
Const	4.2376***	2.6664***	3.6863***	2.6566***	1.5457***	1.6623***	1.5699***	1.7128***	1.7040***
	(0.4200)	(0.2762)	(0.5252)	(0.2812)	(0.0749)	(0.0983)	(0.0971)	(0.2943)	(0.2986)
Female labor participation rate	−0.0136***	0.0026*	0.0018	0.0020	0.0011	−0.0001	0.0008	0.0016	0.0012
	(0.0015)	(0.0014)	(0.0014)	(0.0014)	(0.0011)	(0.0013)	(0.0010)	(0.0013)	(0.0013)
Female unemployment rate	−0.0246***	−0.0157***	−0.0170***	−0.0157***	−0.0108***	−0.0101***	−0.0109***	−0.0112***	−0.0112***
	(0.0031)	(0.0018)	(0.0018)	(0.0017)	(0.0017)	(0.0017)	(0.0016)	(0.0018)	(0.0018)
GDP per capita (logarithm)	−0.1600***	−0.1099***	−0.1967***	−0.1053***	–	–	–	−0.0190	−0.0153
	(0.0431)	(0.0313)	(0.0492)	(0.0309)	–	–	–	(0.0324)	(0.0320)
GDP growth rate	–	–	–	–	0.4995***	0.6081***	0.5020***	0.4853***	0.4904***
	–	–	–	–	(0.0600)	(0.0636)	(0.0600)	(0.0648)	(0.0647)
Social expenditure (total)	0.1581***	0.0563***	0.0354**	0.0582***	0.0617***	0.0399***	0.0633***	0.0619***	0.0635***
	(0.0168)	(0.0143)	(0.0144)	(0.0140)	(0.0137)	(0.0135)	(0.0135)	(0.0137)	(0.0135)
Method	Pooled	Fixed	Fixed	Random	Fixed	Fixed	Random	Fixed	Random
Time dummy	–	No	Yes	No	No	Yes	No	No	No
Hausman statistics	–	–	–	8.3387*	–	-	7.7245	–	7.8301
F statistics	58.01	283.69	187.65	23.94	309.52	210.80	40.23	300.13	32.22
Number of samples	690	690	690	690	690	690	690	690	690
Adj. R^2	0.2487	0.9312	0.9371	0.1175	0.9366	0.9437	0.1855	0.9367	0.1847

Note In the table, *** means 1% significant, **means 5% significant, and * means 10% significant
Standard error in parentheses

Table 3.3 Estimation results by various social expenditure cases

Dependent var: TFR	(1)	(2)	(3)	(4)	(5)	(6)	(7)	(8)
Const	2.6664***	2.7077***	2.7929***	2.3881***	1.5457***	1.4877***	1.5544***	1.5101***
	(0.2762)	(0.2922)	(0.3202)	(0.3319)	(0.0749)	(0.0756)	(0.0777)	(0.0770)
Female labor participation rate	0.0026*	0.0025*	0.0039***	0.0024*	0.0011	0.0024**	0.0024**	0.0017
	(0.0014)	(0.0014)	(0.0014)	(0.0014)	(0.0011)	(0.0010)	(0.0011)	(0.0011)
Female unemployment rate	−0.0157***	−0.0155***	−0.0156***	−0.0158***	−0.0108***	−0.0116***	−0.0105***	−0.0113***
	(0.0018)	(0.0018)	(0.0018)	(0.0018)	(0.0017)	(0.0017)	(0.0017)	(0.0017)
GDP per capita (logarithm)	−0.1099***	−0.0638**	−0.1230***	−0.0819**	–	–	–	–
	(0.0313)	(0.0327)	(0.0353)	(0.0364)	–	–	–	–
GDP growth rate	–	–	–	–	0.4995***	0.4660***	0.4909***	0.4810***
	–	–	–	–	(0.0600)	(0.0599)	(0.0617)	(0.0607)
Social expenditure (total)	0.0563***	–	–	–	0.0617***	–	–	–
	(0.0143)	–	–	–	(0.0137)	–	–	–
Social expenditure (cash)	–	0.0733***	–	0.0729***	–	0.0769***	–	0.0797***
	–	(0.0180)	–	(0.0180)	–	(0.0165)	–	(0.0166)
Social expenditure (in-kind)	–	–	0.0291	0.0273	–	–	0.0200	0.0312
	–	–	(0.0242)	(0.0239)	–	–	(0.0211)	(0.0209)
F statistics	283.69	284.15	277.30	275.96	309.52	310.26	300.09	301.77
Number of samples	690	690	690	690	690	690	690	690
Adj. R^2	0.9312	0.9313	0.9297	0.9314	0.9366	0.9368	0.9347	0.9369

Note In the table, *** means 1% significant, **means 5% significant, and * means 10% significant
Standard error in parentheses. All cases are estimated by fixed effect

of the coefficient of cash benefit are 0.0733 and 0.0729, respectively, and in Cases (6) and (8), the values are 0.0769 and 0.0797, respectively. All estimated coefficients are statistically significant, and the level of the estimated value is the same. However, the estimated value of the in-kind benefit in Cases (3), (4), (7), and (8) is not significant, and the value is relatively small. The meaning of the above results is consistent with the results shown in Table 3.1, derived from simple regression.

In Cases (4) and (8), we observed the estimation results of other variables. The estimated coefficient in Case (4) was 0.0024 and statistically significant at the 10% level for FLP, but smaller. However, we could not obtain a significant value in Case (8). The estimated coefficient of other variables, the FUP and GDPP, was negative, and that of the GDPG was positive, consistent with results in Table 3.2. Thus, the choice of cash benefit is considered preferable for the government policy for improving the TFR.

3.4.3 Dynamic Panel Estimation

While lagged dependent variables have information of current dependent variables, the generalized method of moments (GMM) estimation method estimates them, according to Arellano and Bond (1991). This procedure is called the dynamic panel model. Table 3.4 shows the results of dynamic panel estimation for the TFR using Dataset A. Case (1) is the simplest estimation result, an autoregressive model of order 1. The estimated coefficient of lagged TFR is 0.8735, accounting for almost 99% of the variation of the current TFR.

Cases (2)–(6) contain other independent variables; however, the estimated coefficients of the lagged TFR are almost equal, such as 0.86 to 0.88. Additionally, the FLP, FUR, and SE have a negative estimated coefficient, and it is difficult to explain the sign of results from the hypothesis in the previous section. Particularly, the estimated coefficient of SE is negative and is not statistically significant.

Table 3.5 shows the autoregressive model with TFR of orders 1 to 4. The estimation result of Case (1), that is, the AR (1) model, is shown in Table 3.4. Cases (2) and (4) show the AR (2) and AR (4) models, respectively, and the sum of lagged coefficient of TFR is over unity in both cases. Therefore, it is suggested that the TFR series contain a unit root. This will be confirmed later in the study.

3.4.4 Short-Term Balanced Panel with More Explanatory Variables

Using Dataset C, we explore the effect of more social, political, and demographical factors on the TFR in OECD countries. As the sample countries and periods are restricted, it is difficult to collect more explanatory variables for the 14 countries

Table 3.4 Estimation results of dynamic panel

Dependent var: TFR						
	(1)	(2)	(3)	(4)	(5)	(6)
Const	0.2125***	−0.0259	−0.1992	0.0914	−0.2320	0.0518
	(0.0326)	(0.1294)	(0.1396)	(0.1285)	(0.1423)	(0.1361)
TFR (−1)	0.8735***	0.8746***	0.8791***	0.8609***	0.8841***	0.8652***
	(0.0191)	(0.0190)	(0.0188)	(0.0190)	(0.0193)	(0.0197)
Female labor participation rate	–	–	−0.0019***	–	−0.0017**	–
	–	–	(0.0006)	–	(0.0007)	–
Female unemployment rate	–	–	–	-0.0039***	–	-0.0038***
	–	–	–	(0.0008)	–	(0.0009)
GDP per capita (logarithm)	–	0.0225**	0.0520***	0.0168	0.0545***	0.0206
	–	(0.0120)	(0.0153)	(0.0117)	(0.0155)	(0.0126)
Social expenditure (total)	–	–	–	–	−0.0102	−0.0073
	–	–	–	–	(0.0081)	(0.0077)
Estimation method	GMM	GMM	GMM	GMM	GMM	GMM
Number of samples	630	630	630	630	630	630
Adj. R^2	0.9875	0.9876	0.9878	0.9883	0.9876	0.9882

Note In the table, *** means 1% significant, **means 5% significant, and * means 10% significant
Standard error in parentheses

from 2001 to 2016 than Dataset A. Table 3.6 summarizes the results. In Table 3.6, we added explanatory variables, the share of part-time jobs (PJ), the wage difference between male and female (WD), the average length of maternity and parental leave (MPL), ratio of the child born out of wedlock (BOW), and ratio of females aged 20–49 years to total female population (FPR).

In Cases (1)–(4), while explanatory variables are the same, the estimation method is different, such as pooling model, fixed-effect model without and with time dummy, and random effect model. Although for Case (4), the random effect model is chosen considering statistical test values of the Hausman test and F test, we explore Cases (4) and (2) using the fixed-effect model. The time dummy did not explicitly affect estimation results in Case (4) compared to Cases (2) and (3). In Cases (2) and (4), all explanatory variables have statistically significant coefficients, and the estimated values are almost the same. As for the FLP, the estimated coefficient is positive and different from the results presented in Vol. 1, Table 3.2. Additionally, the GDPG and SE positively impact the TFR. The estimated coefficients of the marginal product of labor (MPL) are negative and significant, suggesting that the length of parental leave does not positively affect the decision to have children by young families.

Table 3.5 Estimation results of panel AR model

Dependent var: TFR				
	(1)	(2)	(3)	(4)
Const	0.2125***	−0.1360	0.1491**	−0.2663
	(0.0326)	(0.1374)	(0.0598)	(0.3205)
TFR (−1)	0.8735***	2.6842***	1.3677***	2.9407***
	(0.0191)	(0.6282)	(0.2137)	(1.1377)
TFR (−2)	–	−1.6040***	−0.2922	−1.7888*
	–	−0.5559	(0.2162)	(1.0821)
TFR (−3)	–	–	-0.1634***	−0.3244*
	–	–	(0.0519)	(0.1777)
TFR (−4)	–	–	–	0.3277
	–	–	–	(0.2543)
Estimation method	GMM	GMM	GMM	GMM
Number of samples	630	600	570	540
Adj. R^2	0.9875	0.9538	0.9857	0.9390

Note In the table, *** means 1% significant, **means 5% significant, and * means 10% significant
Standard error in parentheses

Cases (6) and (8) are estimated using the fixed-effect and random effect models. The PJ, WD, and BOW were added to Cases (2) and (4) as explanatory variables. The FLP, GDPG, and SE have the same impact as in the above cases. However, PJ has negative and statistically significant coefficients. Although part-time job workers are, in principle, more flexible to make arrangements during child-rearing, the following reason may account for this negative impact. Except for some high-powered professionals, part-time job workers are more likely to be at the bottom of the income distribution (i.e., lower-income earners), facing more income uncertainty, and cannot exploit the benefit as full-time workers. Furthermore, WD has a negative sign for the coefficient, which is difficult to interpret. The widening WD means the working environment for females is relatively poor, considered an inadequate work/life balance. Therefore, the wage difference negatively impacts TFR, and the BOW has a positive relationship with TFR.

Furthermore, in Cases (9)–(12), we added more variables such as FUR and GDPP, and the estimation results did not change. In Cases (10) and (12), the FUR had a negative and significant estimated coefficient, but the GDPP did not. Although Case (13) was chosen using the Hausman test statistics, the estimation results of Cases (13) and (15) were similar. The FPR is added as a demographic factor in Cases (13) to (15). The estimated coefficient of FRP is positive and significant, and the value is 2.89 in Case (13) and 2.30 in Case (15). The results of the explanatory variables are the same as observed in previous cases.

Table 3.6 Estimation results with policy variables

Dependent var: TFR								
	(1)	(2)	(3)	(4)	(5)	(6)	(7)	(8)
Const	0.3018	0.4330**	0.3260	0.4444**	1.4452***	1.1276***	0.5665*	1.1444***
	(0.1959)	(0.2145)	(0.2460)	(0.2149)	(0.2438)	(0.2422)	(0.2993)	(0.2347)
Female labor participation rate	0.0169***	0.0136***	0.0149***	0.0136***	−0.0017	0.0185***	0.0177***	0.0170***
	(0.0028)	(0.0029)	(0.0032)	(0.0028)	(0.0036)	(0.0037)	(0.0032)	(0.0035)
Female unemployment rate	–	–	–	–	–	–	–	–
	–	–	–	–	–	–	–	–
Share of part-time job	–	–	–	–	−0.0072***	−0.0046	−0.0071***	−0.0058**
	–	–	–	–	(0.0015)	(0.0031)	(0.0026)	(0.0025)
Wage difference	–	–	–	–	0.0031	−0.0157***	−0.0071**	−0.0132***
	–	–	–	–	(0.0025)	(0.0034)	(0.0026)	(0.0032)
GDP per capita (logarithm)	–	–	–	–	–	–	–	–
	–	–	–	–	–	–	–	–
GDP growth rate	0.8528**	0.5597***	0.7530***	0.5463***	−0.2547	0.6782***	0.9355***	0.6625***
	(0.4264)	(0.1907)	(0.2286)	(0.1890)	(0.3557)	(0.1810)	(0.2180)	(0.1784)
Social expenditure (total)	0.0923***	0.1539***	0.1652***	0.1491***	0.0535**	0.1755***	0.1799***	0.1648***
	(0.0176)	(0.0218)	(0.0202)	(0.0209)	(0.0230)	(0.0216)	(0.0193)	(0.0207)
Maternity and parental leave	−0.0034***	−0.0033***	−0.0038***	−0.0033***	−0.0030***	−0.0029***	−0.0035***	−0.0032***
	(0.0003)	(0.0005)	(0.0004)	(0.0005)	(0.0004)	(0.0005)	(0.0005)	(0.0005)
Child born out of wedlock	–	–	–	–	0.0089***	0.0060***	0.0060***	0.0054***
	–	–	–	–	(0.0020)	(0.0017)	(0.0017)	(0.0016)

(continued)

Table 3.6 (continued)

Dependent var: TFR	(1)	(2)	(3)	(4)	(5)	(6)	(7)	(8)
Female 2049 ratio	–	–	–	–	–	–	–	–
	–	–	–	–	–	–	–	–
Method	Pooled	Fixed	Fixed	Random	Pooled	Fixed	Fixed	Random
Time dummy	–	No	Yes	No	–	No	Yes	No
Human statistics	–	–	–	1.0080	–	–	–	10.3640
F statistics	63.215	199.31	157.40	38.713	75.644	193.54	163.26	29.312
Number of samples	224	224	224	224	224	224	224	224
Adj. R^2	0.5274	0.9380	0.9573	0.4035	0.7009	0.9453	0.9622	0.4705

Dependent var: TFR	(9)	(10)	(11)	(12)	(13)	(14)	(15)
Const	−0.4844	0.6870	−0.9982	0.7311	−2.8036***	−1.2147	−2.1059**
	(0.7337)	(0.6858)	(1.0664)	(0.6420)	(0.9089)	(1.0754)	(0.8574)
Female labor participation rate	−0.0045	0.0168***	0.0161***	0.0150***	0.0189***	0.0167***	0.0170***
	(0.0038)	(0.0038)	(0.0032)	(0.0037)	(0.0036)	(0.0032)	(0.0035)
Female unemployment rate	−0.0042	−0.0111**	−0.0089**	−0.0107**	−0.0138***	−0.0104**	−0.0124***
	(0.0064)	(0.0047)	(0.0042)	(0.0046)	(0.0044)	(0.0043)	(0.0043)
Share of part-time job	−0.0082***	−0.0033	−0.0057**	−0.0047*	0.0013	−0.0043	−0.0023
	(0.0015)	(0.0031)	(0.0026)	(0.0026)	(0.0030)	(0.0028)	(0.0025)
Wage difference	0.0049**	−0.0143***	−0.0048	−0.0122***	−0.0010***	−0.0055	−0.0089***

(continued)

Table 3.6 (continued)

Dependent var: TFR							
	(9)	(10)	(11)	(12)	(13)	(14)	(15)
	(0.0025)	(0.0034)	(0.0033)	(0.0033)	(0.0033)	(0.0033)	(0.0031)
GDP per capita (logarithm)	0.1933***	0.0543	0.1433	0.0500	0.2018***	0.1290	0.1796***
	(0.0718)	(0.0732)	(0.0909)	(0.0674)	(0.0737)	(0.0913)	(0.0682)
GDP growth rate	−0.2240	0.5832***	0.7643***	0.5832***	0.4693***	0.7555***	0.4642***
	(0.3618)	(0.1836)	(0.2218)	(0.1797)	(0.1734)	(0.2213)	(0.1694)
Social expenditure (total)	0.0762***	0.1723***	0.1794***	0.1638***	0.1808***	0.1769***	0.1647***
	(0.0246)	(0.0215)	(0.0193)	(0.0206)	(0.0201)	(0.0193)	(0.0191)
Maternity and parental leave	−0.0028***	−0.0025***	−0.0031***	−0.0028***	−0.0016***	−0.0028***	−0.0023***
	(0.0004)	(0.0005)	(0.0005)	(0.0005)	(0.0005)	(0.0005)	(0.0005)
Child born out of wedlock	0.0071***	0.0048***	0.0054***	0.0046***	0.0063***	0.0053***	0.0051***
	(0.0021)	(0.0018)	(0.0016)	(0.0017)	(0.0017)	(0.0016)	(0.0015)
Female 2049 ratio	–	–	–	–	2.8900***	0.8591	2.2966***
	–	–	–	–	(0.5327)	(0.6244)	(0.5011)
Method	Pooled	Fixed	Fixed	Random	Fixed	Fixed	Random
Time dummy	–	No	Yes	No	No	Yes	No
Hausman statistics	–	–	–	10.497	–	–	26.370***
F statistics	63.121	180.43	160.31	23.99	198.28	156.89	25.48
Number of samples	224	224	224	224	224	224	224
Adj.R^2	0.7149	0.9465	0.9635	0.4812	0.9532	0.9637	0.5233

Note In the table, *** means 1% significant, **means 5% significant, and * means 10% significant
Standard error in parentheses

3.5 Nonstationary of Data and Panel Analysis

As the panel data consist of time series data, confirming the data generating process is necessary to analyze them; data stationarity is a required characteristic. Therefore, a panel unit root test on our dataset is required. When the unit root is observed in the dataset, a panel cointegration test or an estimation using the difference series should be implemented.

3.5.1 *Pane Unit Root Test and Cointegration Test*

As the ratio of the power of unit root test to individual time series is weak, a panel unit root test is utilized to compensate for the test power. There are two generations of tests within the panel unit root test: the first-generation tests and the second-generation tests. First-generation tests presume that cross-sectional units are independent. The IPS test, Fisher ADF test, Fisher PP test, and LLC test are classified as the first-generation test. However, second-generation tests assume the correlation among cross-sectional units. The CPIS test or CD test is included in the second generation. Details about panel unit root tests are as given, for example, Baltagi (2005).

Considering the data characteristics in this study, we adopted the first-generation unit root tests. Table 3.7 shows the results of panel unit root tests on Dataset B, concluding the longest period data. Although several countries included in this dataset are restricted, this conclusion could be applied to another Dataset A in the case of a unit root.

We implemented four kinds of unit root tests, the IPS, Fischer ADF, PP, and LLC tests, to six main variables, such as the TFR, FLP, GDPP, and social expenditures (SEs). We chose the Schwarz information criterion as a basic reference while determining the lag degree of each test. First, we tested these variables for level series. Although the Fischer PP and LLC tests rejected the null hypothesis, they do not contain a unit root; the IPS and Fischer ADF tests did not reject the null hypothesis, as they contain a unit root. Based on these tests, we concluded unit root existed in the six variables. Therefore, unit root tests were conducted to the first-order difference series of the six variables. Table 3.7 shows that the null hypothesis was rejected; therefore, we concluded that the first difference series were stationary.

When the unit root in level series is confirmed, the panel cointegration test must confirm long-term equilibrium among the concerned variables. There are two types of cointegration tests: residual-based test and system test. We used a residual-based cointegration test for the TFR, FLP, GDPP, and SE, and all tests excluding the panel ADF test rejected the existence of cointegration, as shown in Table 3.8. Hence, we construct the model using the first difference series.

Table 3.7 Results of panel unit root test

	IPS test	Fisher ADF	Fisher PP	LLC test	
Level series					
TFR	0.5332	65.551	74.843*	−1.5808*	4
Female labor participation rate	0.3419	72.220	137.638***	−5.8634***	2
GDP per capita (logarithm)	−0.3431	68.947	84.872**	−4.7865***	4
Social expenditure (total)	−0.3212	73.537	82.594**	−1.4708*	2
Social expenditure (cash)	−0.1456	114.38***	94.774***	−3.4569***	4
Social expenditure (in-kind)	−1.6234*	140.99***	101.35***	−3.0480***	4
Differenced series					
TFR	−9.9342***	231.43***	309.11***	−5.7437***	4
Female labor participation rate	−16.045***	338.86***	370.53***	−17.657***	4
GDP per capita (logarithm)	−14.74***	311.77***	319.85***	−16.006***	4
Social expenditure (total)	−14.171***	306.79***	348.73***	−15.808***	4
Social expenditure (cash)	−12.885***	299.90***	341.58***	−13.526***	4
Social expenditure (in-kind)	−15.635***	337.03***	387.80***	−17.410***	4

Note Sample period is 1986–2017, and lag degree was determined by Schwarz information criterion

Table 3.8 Results of panel cointegration test

	Statistic	Prob
Panel v statistic	1.2499	0.1057
Panel rho statistic	1.0355	0.8498
Panel PP statistic	−1.2133	0.1125
Panel ADF statistic	−2.8398	0.0023

Note Sample period is 1986–2017

3.5.2 *Difference Series and Estimation Results*

Based on the conclusions of the previous subsection, the difference series of each variable is required to estimate the impact of socioeconomic factors on the TFR. We chose three main variables as explanatory factors and classified the total social expenditure into cash and in-kind benefits. Table 3.9 shows the results for difference

Table 3.9 Estimation results of difference series of panel data

Dependent var: D_TFR								
	(1)	(2)	(3)	(4)	(5)	(6)	(7)	(8)
Const	-0.0057**	-0.0075***	-0.0055**	-0.0100***	-0.0086***	-0.0085***	-0.0081***	-0.0091***
	(0.0020)	(0.0023)	(0.0024)	(0.0023)	(0.0025)	(0.0022)	(0.0024)	(0.0023)
D_Female labor participation rate	0.0050**	0.0048**	0.0021	0.0053**	0.0025	0.0054**	0.0048**	0.0054**
	(0.0023)	(0.0023)	(0.0019)	(0.0023)	(0.0019)	(0.0022)	(0.0023)	(0.0022)
D_GDP per capita (logarithm)	–	0.0761*	0.0333	0.1347***	0.0986*	0.1309***	0.0827*	0.1366***
	–	(0.0451)	(0.0498)	(0.0457)	(0.0505)	(0.0451)	(0.0455)	(0.0455)
D_Social expenditure (total)	–	–	–	0.0600***	0.0581***	–	–	–
	–	–	–	(0.0118)	(0.0181)	–	–	–
D_Social expenditure (cash)	–	–	–	–	–	0.0809***	–	0.0806***
	–	–	–	–	–	(0.0146)	–	(0.0146)
D_Social expenditure (in-kind)	–	–	–	–	–	–	0.0220	0.0196
	–	–	–	–	–	–	(0.0210)	(0.0205)
F statistics	1.846	1.884	1.036	2.703	2.237	2.875	1.859	2.815
Number of samples	660	660	576	660	576	660	660	660
Number of countries	30	30	18	30	18	30	30	30
Periods	1996–2017	1996–2017	1986–2017	1996–2017	1986–2017	1996–2017	1996–2017	1996–2017
Adj. R^2	0.0371	0.0399	0.0012	0.0764	0.04124	0.0834	0.0401	0.0833

Note In the table, *** means 1% significant, **means 5% significant, and * means 10% significant
Standard error in parentheses

panel data. The fixed-effect model estimates all cases. Hereafter, the variables in the difference series are described as D_TFR, D_FLP, D_GDPP, and D_SEs.

The results from Cases (3) and (5) were obtained using Dataset B, covering the longest period. However, several countries are restricted in Dataset B, and the results for the other cases were obtained using Dataset A, which includes 30 countries covering marginally shorter periods. In cases that used Dataset A, the D_FLP positively and significantly impacted the TFR. D_GDPP positively affected the D_TFR, except in Case (3). This is consistent with the previous estimation results because difference series of GDP per capita in logarithm means per capita economic growth rate. However, the results for the impacts of D_SE are notable. The estimated coefficient of D_SE (total) is positive and statistically significant in Case (4). Additionally, the D_SE (cash) is positive and statistically significant in Cases (6) and (8). However, the impact of D_SE (in-kind) does not have a statistically significant effect on D_TFR in Cases (7) and (8). Overall, we reconfirmed the positive effects of social expenditure on young families by the government. Particularly, a cash benefit seemed more effective from the above estimation results.

Although it has been highlighted that the information contained in the level variables cannot be fully utilized in the difference series, considering the time series characteristics is essential for the difference series. Evaluating this discussion is a difficult problem. However, it is considered that the same implications indicated by the results in the previous section were obtained from the estimation results of the difference series.

3.6 Conclusions

This study explores the relationship between the TFR and socioeconomic factors, such as the labor market, macroeconomic environments, political tools, and demographic conditions. Therefore, three balanced panel datasets consisting of OECD countries were used.

Initially, confirming the effect of the government support using social expenditure on young families positively and significantly impacts the TFR. Furthermore, classifying this expenditure to cash benefit and in-kind benefit shows that the in-kind benefit positively impacts the pooling model. However, a cash benefit is effective in the fixed-effect model.

Although the FLP correlates positively with the TFR in the simple pooling model, the empirical results using Dataset A did not show statistical significance in the fixed-effect model with more explanatory variables. However, the female unemployment rate negatively impacts the TFR and is statistically significant in all cases. As for the macroeconomic environment, the level of GDP per capita is negative. However, the economic growth rate positively affects the TFR. This result may be interpreted as the expectation of the economic environment in future works, improving the decision to have children. Furthermore, the estimated coefficient of the MPL has a negative sign. However, social expenditure has a positive influence on the TFR.

Lastly, the demographic variable, that is, the young female population ratio to the total population and the ratio of a child born out of wedlock, shows a positive estimated coefficient.

Additionally, we estimated the dynamic panel model. The lagged variable of TFR explains the current TFR. Therefore, to estimate the AR model, it is required to show the time series characteristics. More concretely, stationarity is necessary to estimate the time series model. Confirming the unit root test for the main variables, we concluded that these variables contain a unit root, and there is no cointegration among them. Therefore, we confirmed the same conclusions as in the previous result in the case of level variables, using a difference series.

This study contributes to related fields as follows. First, although there was similar empirical research using panel data of developed countries by various researchers, as summarized in the previous section, we added the more detailed related variables, including policy tools. We distinguished the impacts of a cash benefit and in-kind benefit; we showed the impact of the macroeconomic environment on the TFR. Second, we estimated a difference panel data model responding to the empirical findings that the variables contain a unit root. Therefore, we identified the same positive impact of economic growth rate and social expenditure by the government as in the level variable cases.

Topics for future research are as follows: 1) further confirmation of policy effects to improve the TFR by constructing datasets with longer-term and abundant variables, especially the re-verification of the effects of in-kind benefits, 2) verification of different situations between Asian countries and developed Western countries using a similar panel data model, and 3) examination of other approaches using the variable results of time series characteristics.

Appendix Lists of Countries in Dataset

Dataset A (30 countries, 1995–2017).

Australia, Austria, Belgium, Canada, Czech Republic, Denmark, Finland, France, Germany, Greece, Iceland, Ireland, Israel, Italy, Japan, Korea, Luxembourg, Mexico, Netherlands, New Zealand, Norway, Poland, Portugal, Slovak Republic, Spain, Sweden, Switzerland, Turkey, UK, and USA.

Dataset B (18 countries, 1985–2017).

Australia, Belgium, Canada, Denmark, Finland, France, Germany, Greece, Ireland, Italy, Japan, Luxembourg, Netherlands, Portugal, Spain, Sweden, UK, and USA.

Dataset C (14 countries, 2001–2016).

Austria, Belgium, Canada, Czech Republic, Finland, France, Germany, Japan, Korea, New Zealand, Norway, Sweden, UK, and USA.

References

Adserá, A. (2004). Changing fertility rates in developed countries. The impact of labor market institutions. *Journal of Population Economics, 17*(1), 17–43.

Arellano, M., & Bond, S. (1991). Some tests of specification for panel data: Monte Carlo evidence and an application to employment equations. *Review of Economic Studies, 58*(2), 277–297.

Baltagi, B. (2005). *Econometric analysis of panel data* (3rd ed.). Wiley.

Castles, F. G. (2003). The world turned upside down: Below replacement fertility, changing preferences and family-friendly public policy in 21 OECD countries. *Journal of European Social Policy, 13*(3), 209–227.

D'Addio, A.C., & D'Ercole, M.M. (2005). *Trends and determinants of fertility rates: The role of policies*. OECD Working Paper 27, OECD.

Gauthier, A. H., & Hatzius, J. (1997). Family benefits and fertility: An econometric analysis. *Population Studies, 51*(3), 295–306.

Hondroyiannis, G. (2010). Fertility determinants and economic uncertainty: An assessment using European panel data. Bank of Greece Working Paper No. 96. *Journal of Family and Economic Issues, 31*(1), 33–50.

Kato, H. (2011). Intergenerational inequlity, Chikuma-Shinsho, No. 930, Chikuma-Shobo. (in Japanese).

Lechman, E., Dominiak, P., & Okonowicz, A. (2014). Fertility rebound and economic growth. New evidence for 18 countries over the period 1970–2011, MPRA Paper No. 55104.

Luci-Greulich, A., & Thévenon, O. (2013). The impact of family policies on fertility trends in developed countries. *European Journal of Population/Revue Européenne De Démographie, 29*(4), 387–416.

Olivetti, C., & Petrongolo, B. (2017). The economic consequences of family policies: lessons from a century of legislation in high-income countries. IZA Institute of Labor Economics, Discussion Paper Series, vol. IZA DP No, 10505.

Rovny, A. E. (2011). Welfare state policy determinants of fertility level: A comparative analysis. *Journal of European Social Policy, 21*(4), 335–347.

Thévenon, O. (2011). Family policies in OECD countries: A comparative analysis. *Population and Development Review, 37*(1), 57–87.

The manufacturer's authorised representative in the EU is Springer Nature Customer Service Centre GmbH, Europaplatz 3, 69115 Heidelberg, Germany. If you have any concerns regarding our products, please contact ProductSafety@springernature.com

Printed and bound by CPI Group (UK) Ltd, Croydon, CR0 4YY
30/09/2026
02225261-0005